"This book offers a comprehensive and insightful contribution to understanding transformations experienced in the institutes of consecrated life in the United States and globally. It is unique in that most of the chapters articulate the realities of aging members and the cultural and ethnic diversity of the emerging religious institutes. The book documents thoughtful reflections, learnings, and innovative ways religious institutes are reimaging new structures for mission and charism, including discernment processes and new governance and collaborative models. It invites us into the emerging creative field of research on consecrated life. Regardless of the challenges facing religious life today, this book affirms the core tenet of consecrated women's fidelity to God and pragmatic listening to contemporary challenges as an opportunity to learn and respond to new realities with new possibilities, hope, wisdom, and grace."

—Sister Jane Wakahiu, LSOSF, Associate Vice President of
Programs Operations and Head Catholic Sisters Initiative
at the Conrad N. Hilton Foundation

New Faces, New Possibilities

Cultural Diversity and Structural Change in Institutes of Women Religious

Center for Applied Research in the Apostolate

Edited by

Thomas P. Gaunt, SJ, and Thu T. Do, LHC

LITURGICAL PRESS ACADEMIC

Collegeville, Minnesota
www.litpress.org

1   2   3   4   5   6   7   8   9

Library of Congress Cataloging-in-Publication Data

Names: Gaunt, Thomas P., editor. | Do, Thu (Thu T.), editor. | Center for Applied Research in the Apostolate (U.S.)

Title: New faces, new possibilities : cultural diversity and structural change in institutes of women religious / Center for Applied Research in the Apostolate ; edited by Thomas P. Gaunt, SJ and Thu T. Do, LHC.

Description: Collegeville, Minnesota : Liturgical Press Academic, [2022] | Includes bibliographical references and index. | Summary: "This book examines the changes in culture and ethnicity among religious sisters in the United States, the structural impact of diminishing numbers, and the creative response to this new reality for religious life in the United States. In it, sisters from a variety of generations, cultures, and institutes join with CARA researchers to examine and reflect on CARA's recent research findings and their impact on the life and ministry of sisters today"— Provided by publisher.

Identifiers: LCCN 2021051515 (print) | LCCN 2021051516 (ebook) | ISBN 9780814667392 (paperback) | ISBN 9780814667408 (epub) | ISBN 9780814667408 (pdf)

Subjects: LCSH: Monasticism and religious orders for women—United States—History—21st century.

Classification: LCC BX4220.U6 N49 2022 (print) | LCC BX4220.U6 (ebook) | DDC 271.90073—dc23/eng/20220105

LC record available at https://lccn.loc.gov/2021051515

LC ebook record available at https://lccn.loc.gov/2021051516

Contents

Figures

Tables

Contributors

Maria Theotokos Adams is a member of the Servants of the Lord and of the Virgin of Matará, the female branch of the Religious Family of the Incarnate Word (IVE). She is currently completing her doctoral studies in Church history at The Catholic University of America in Washington, DC. Her religious institute was founded in 1988 in Argentina and now has more than 1,350 members in over thirty-five countries.

Patricia Cormack is on the leadership team of the Holy Cross Sisters–USA Province. She is the board president of the Wisconsin Religious Collaborative, an organization designed to allow the nine participating religious institutes to assist each other in providing needed internal management services through collaboration, sharing of personnel or programs, or seeking and/or sharing the services of outside vendors. It is the first such organization in the United States.

Thu T. Do is a Sister of the Lovers of the Holy Cross of Hanoi from Vietnam. She is currently a research associate at CARA. She is involved in various survey research projects, specializing in the area of religious life. Among her coauthored publications are *Word, Liturgy, Charity: The Diaconate in the US Catholic Church, 1968–2018*; *Pathways to Religious Life*; and *Migration for Mission: International Catholic Sisters in the United States*.

Sharon Euart is a Sister of Mercy of the Americas who holds a doctorate in canon law and is currently the executive director of the Resource Center for Religious Institutes (RCRI) in Silver Spring, Maryland. In the past she has served as the executive coordinator of the Canon Law Society of America and a canonical consultant for religious institutes and diocesan bishops. She also served as associate general secretary to the United States Conference of Catholic Bishops.

Thomas P. Gaunt is a Jesuit priest and executive director of CARA. He has served in Jesuit governance as the socius/executive secretary of the Jesuit Conference–USA and was the formation and studies director of the Maryland and New York Jesuit Provinces. After ordination, he spent ten years as a pastor and as director of planning and research in the Diocese of Charlotte. He has coauthored or edited three books at CARA, including *Catholic Parishes of the 21ˢᵗ Century*; *Pathways to Religious Life*; and *Catholic Bishops in the United States: Church Leadership in the Third Millennium*.

Mary L. Gautier is a sociologist and retired senior research associate at CARA, where she specialized in Catholic demographic trends in the United States. She edited *The CARA Report* and other CARA publications. She is coauthor of twelve books on US Catholicism, most recently, *Migration for Mission: International Catholic Sisters in the United States*.

Mumbi Kigutha is a member of the Sisters of the Precious Blood–Ohio. She is a native of Kenya. Based in Chicago, Illinois, she ministers as the organizing secretary for the Pan-African Catholic Theology and Pastoral Network and as a part-time consultant for Jesuit Refugee Service; she regularly contributes to the *Global Sisters Report* and other publications.

Michal Kramarek is a research associate at CARA. He conducts primarily diocesan-level and national-level studies on men and women religious in the United States and Canada. He is coauthor of *Word, Liturgy, Charity: The Diaconate in the US Catholic Church, 1968–2018.*

Juliet Mousseau is a member of the Society of the Sacred Heart. She holds a PhD in historical theology from Saint Louis University. She serves as the vice president for academic affairs at the Franciscan School of Theology in San Diego, California.

Jonathon L. Wiggins is a sociologist and research associate at CARA who helps mentor religious sisters from the African continent in social scientific research methods through CARA's Visiting Scholar Program. He has coauthored two books: *Catholic Parishes of the 21ˢᵗ Century* and *Word, Liturgy, Charity: The Diaconate in the US Catholic Church, 1968–2018.*

Patricia Wittberg is a Sister of Charity of Cincinnati, Ohio. She holds a PhD in sociology from the University of Chicago and is currently a research associate with CARA. She is the author of numerous books and articles on Catholicism and Catholic religious life, most recently, *Migration for Mission: International Catholic Sisters in the United States.*

INTRODUCTION

Thomas P. Gaunt

Why Are Catholic Sisters Important Today?

The first group of Catholic Sisters (Ursulines) to live and minister in what is today the United States arrived in 1727 in the city of New Orleans, which was then a French colony, and soon thereafter opened a school and a hospital. By the late 1700s, after the American Revolution, Carmelite and Visitation Sisters were established in Maryland and the District of Columbia. Year by year, the number of sisters and their religious institutes continued to increase in number such that by 1850 there were more than 1,300 sisters and over 40,000 by 1900.[1] Overwhelmingly, the women entering religious life were immigrants or the daughters of immigrants who had come to the United States from Europe, bringing with them the popular piety and devotions of their homelands (France, Germany, Ireland, Italy, etc.) and most typically serving their fellow immigrants in ministries of health care, social service, and education. The number of Catholics during the nineteenth century grew faster than the number of clergy who could serve them. Several historians claim that the sisters were therefore more effective than the bishops and priests in meeting

---

1. Patricia Wittberg, *The Rise and Fall of Catholic Religious Orders: A Social Movement Perspective* (Albany: SUNY Press, 1994), 39.

the challenges of preserving and fostering the Catholic faith.[2] In addition, the nursing services of the sisters, especially during the Civil War, were largely responsible for destroying anti-Catholic prejudice in the United States for a generation.[3]

The ministries of education and health care framed much of what the earliest sisters did and set the stage for their creation of the largest nonpublic education and healthcare systems in the United States, from which millions of Catholics and non-Catholics have benefited for nearly three centuries. During this time, sisters have kept the faith alive and engaged in community after community through education, works of charity, and advocacy for families and individuals on the margins of society (e.g., immigrants, orphans, and those suffering impoverishment). By 1965, the peak year for the number of sisters in the United States, there were more than 180,000 sisters.

In the late 1960s, following the Second Vatican Council and in a time of great social change and turmoil in the United States, the number of sisters began a sharp decline. This decline was in part due to a large number of sisters who left religious life in the 1970s and 1980s but also due to a much smaller number who were entering religious life. As a result, by 2020, there were about 45,000 sisters in the United States, and most of them were at or beyond retirement age.

Yet women continue to enter religious life. There are about two hundred younger women entering a religious institute in the United States each year. The religious institutes that they enter generally have a majority of members who are seventy-five years of age or older. Adult American Catholics are largely aware that the elderly sisters who once taught them and cared for them in

---

2. Mary Ewens, "Women in the Convent," in *American Catholic Women: A Historical Exploration,* ed. Karen Kennelly (New York: Macmillan, 1989), 17–47; Michael E. Engh, *Frontier Faiths: Church, Temple, and Synagogue in Los Angeles, 1846–1888* (Albuquerque: University of New Mexico Press, 1992), 141.

3. Ewens, "Women in the Convent," 26.

their youth are rapidly diminishing in number. But they are often unaware of the hundreds of younger women who are entering religious life each year, much less of the thousands of sisters living and ministering in the United States who have come from other countries.

An all too common narrative among American Catholics in 2020 is that the sisters have aged out and are disappearing from the Church's life and ministry, with minimal awareness of the new and renewed communities of religious women emerging across the country. In 2019 America Media, in collaboration with the Center for Applied Research in the Apostolate (CARA), produced a series of videos highlighting the history of Catholic sisters in the United States and presenting four short vignettes of young sisters speaking about their vocation and call to service in the Church today. This series of brief YouTube videos (https://www.youtube.com /watch?v=83yZNrXOH1k) captures well how sisters went to the frontiers in the nineteenth and early twentieth centuries, creating much of the ministry and outreach of the Catholic Church then, and how sisters (though presently fewer in number) are doing the same today.

During the past five years, a great deal of CARA research has focused on the life and ministry of sisters in the United States. This research gathered data on the women who are responding to the call to religious life at the beginning of the twenty-first century, their cultural and ethnic diversity, and the number who are coming to the United States from other nations, along with the emergence of new religious institutes over the years. Recent CARA research has also focused on the evolution of leadership within religious institutes, the transformation of institute governance structures, and the expansion of collaboration in institutional ministries. Sisters continue to be critical to the life of the Catholic Church, yet "who" the sisters are and "how" they serve has evolved.

This short book is divided into two sections: New Waves of Women Religious and Changes in Governance and Collaboration. The first section begins with an examination of who is entering religious life in recent years in chapter 1, followed by a look at the cultural and ethnic diversity of these new members in contrast to the elder sisters in their religious institutes in chapter 2. Chapter 3 details the increasing number of religious institutes with a presence in the United States that were founded and formed in Africa, Asia, and Latin America—very different cultural and religious contexts from North America and Europe—and describes how these international sisters are changing the face of religious life in the United States. This first section concludes with a pair of essays by newer sisters reflecting on these transformations and the ways they are challenging women's religious institutes in the United States.

The second section presents CARA data on the changes in governance and collaboration in ministry that are occurring among so many religious institutes in recent years. A number of religious institutes that were founded in the United States in the nineteenth and early twentieth centuries established missions in other countries around the world many years ago. As those mission institutes flourished while the sending institutes received few or no new members, these institutes now have most of their active sisters and leadership pool outside of the United States. How do these institutes evolve to reflect this reality? Quite practically, how do they transfer their governance from the United States to the mission country, perhaps Korea or India? How does this transfer change the relationship of who is dependent on whom? These challenges are presented in chapter 5. Chapter 6 examines the demographic realities confronting many US-based religious institutes as their members over age seventy-five now far outnumber those who are younger. Do they have enough active younger members to sustain their governance? Over the past two centuries, sisters have evolved and adapted the governance structures of their religious institutes to better respond to their life and mission. How do they now renew their governance to best serve a diminishing number of members and the possibility of completion? These questions are examined in chapter 7. The second section concludes with two essays reflecting on the practical and current experience of a community leader addressing diminishment and a sister of a new growing "missionary" institute.

The book concludes with our learnings about "who" the new women religious are and "how" leadership and governance are evolving in religious life today.

More than two hundred years ago, the first of many thousands of sisters spread out across the United States as they responded to the pressing needs of their time: education, health care, child development, teaching the faith, and fostering devotions among millions of recent immigrants often pushed to the edge of American society. The same work continues today—yet it takes place with a much smaller, more diverse group of women, charisms, and ministries. Are we paying attention? Can we envision the ways sisters will continue to transform the Church in the United States as they have repeatedly done for centuries?

PART

I

New Waves of Women Religious

*Mary L. Gautier and
Thu T. Do*

New Members in Religious Life in the United States

As described in the introduction to this book, something important happened to Catholic religious life in the 1960s in the United States and around the world. *Perfectae Caritatis*, the Decree on the Appropriate Renewal of the Religious Life that was issued by the Second Vatican Council in 1965, had something to do with it. Social conditions of the day such as increasing educational opportunities for women, particularly in the Global North, had something to do with it. In the United States, the successful assimilation of generations of Catholic immigrants into American society had something to do with it. There were many other factors as well that played a part, but the rapid social change of that decade brought to a screeching halt the waves of young Catholics who had been entering religious orders by the thousands, many of them right out of high school, in the 1940s, 1950s, and 1960s. Religious institutes continued to offer vocation talks in Catholic schools and parishes but fewer young people responded. Entrance classes of dozens of young men and women dropped off to just a few. Gradually, religious institutes reported just one or two young people discerning a vocation; many others had no one entering religious life. Something was happening to religious life.

Fast forward fifty years and the effects of the social change that swept through religious life in the 1960s and 1970s are playing out dramatically in religious institutes today. Close to half of the institutes of women religious that existed in the United States just twenty years ago have merged or closed. The average age of members in the remaining institutes is in the high seventies. Yet some women continue to respond to the call to religious life. In the United States, about one to two hundred women enter a religious institute each year, and roughly half of them persist to take perpetual vows some eight years later. They live, pray, and learn about religious life in communities of women that are often many decades older than they. Yet they create community with these much older members and find religious life to be meaningful and fulfilling.

This chapter explores the characteristics of these contemporary women who are entering religious life today. Through annual studies conducted by CARA of those entering religious institutes and of those professing perpetual vows in religious life, a detailed composite portrait emerges from the data of the characteristics, preferences, attitudes, and behaviors of the women who are responding to a call to religious life today.

Who Are the New Members in Religious Life?

A 2019 CARA study[1] of almost 2,000 new members in religious institutes who had entered religious life since 2003, about half of them women, found that the average age of these women at the time of the survey was thirty-seven years old. A similar study, completed ten years previously, reported the average age of new women members in 2009 was forty-four years old. Thus, although the average age of new members appears to be dropping a bit in recent years, these women are still much older than the new members of fifty or sixty years ago who were mostly in their mid-to-late twenties (see figure 1.1).

---

1. See appendix at the end for a more detailed description of this and other CARA studies used in this book.

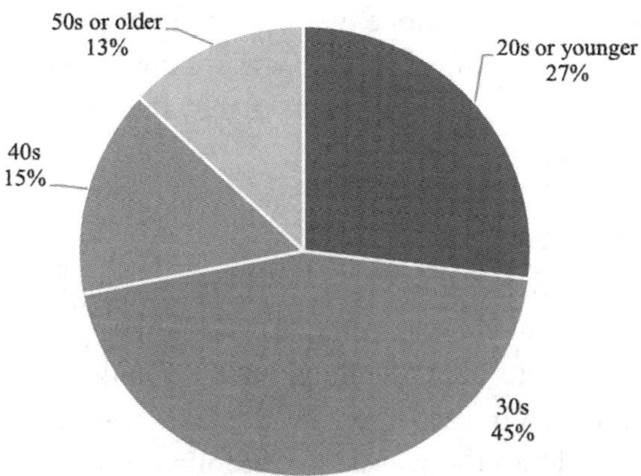

Figure 1.1. Age of new members entering religious institutes since 2003. *Source*: Data from Mary Gautier and Thu Do, *Recent Vocations to Religious Life: A Report for the National Religious Vocation Conference* (Washington, DC: Center for Applied Research in the Apostolate, 2020).

The women who are entering religious life today are not entering right out of high school; rather, they are discerning their vocation for several years while they pursue higher education, earn money in a job, and gain maturity and experience. These women are not fresh-faced teenagers, seeking adventure and opportunity in pursuit of a religious vocation. Today's new women religious are clear-eyed and more realistic in their discernment of a vocation, with education and life experience that have already shaped them.

Similar to new religious of previous generations, fully half of these women first considered a vocation to religious life in childhood. Another quarter first considered this life while they were in college. They entered religious life a decade or two after they first considered it, though, discerning for much longer than the young novices of the 1940s and 1950s, who tended to respond to the call right out of high school. These new religious entered religious life in their late twenties, on average at age twenty-eight, and about half of them persist to perpetual vows after eight to ten years of formation in a religious institute. They take these vows of poverty, chastity, and obedience when they are nearly forty, but fully half of them are age thirty-five or younger when they take these vows. Thus, unlike many in previous generations, these women are more mature, more self-aware, more prepared to freely embrace the vows, and less likely to change their mind about their vocation to religious life.

Race and Ethnicity

Another way that these new members in religious life differ substantially from their counterparts of earlier generations is in their race and ethnicity. While previous generations of women religious came from the largely White European families whose ancestors made up the waves of Catholic immigrants entering the United States in the nineteenth and early twentieth centuries, these newer members are increasingly the children or grandchildren of immigrants from Catholic countries outside of Europe—in Asia, Latin America, and Africa. Thus, their racial and ethnic composition is much more diverse than those of previous generations. This can be most clearly seen in a comparison of the racial and ethnic diversity of fully professed members of religious institutes compared to the racial and ethnic diversity of those in formation, as reported by the religious superiors of these religious institutes (see figures 1.2 and 1.3).

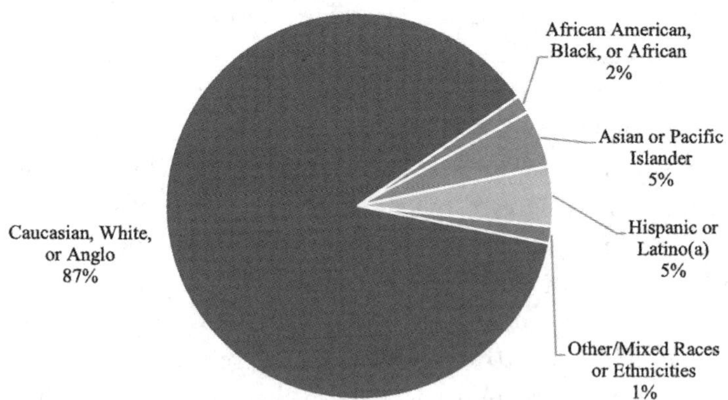

Figure 1.2. Racial and ethnic background of perpetually vowed members. *Source*: Data from Gautier and Do (2020).

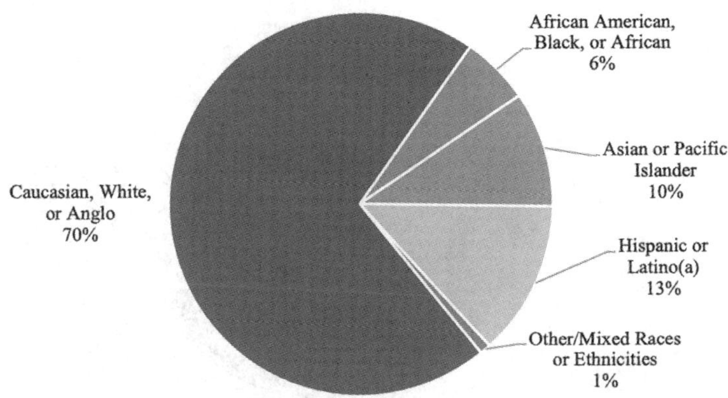

Figure 1.3. Racial and ethnic background of members in initial formation. *Source*: Data from Gautier and Do (2020).

As the United States has become more racially and ethnically diverse, so too has religious life. The implications of this increasing diversity are explored in greater depth in the next chapter, but this chapter illustrates the increased racial and ethnic diversity of newer members of religious institutes of women. As seen in figure 1.3, about seven in ten members in formation are White, compared to nearly nine in ten members who have professed perpetual vows. Religious of color are about 13 percent of full members, while they make up three in ten among members in formation. The implications of this change are broad and far-reaching.

Nativity

These new members are also less likely than other members of religious institutes to be US born—one in five new members of women's institutes was born in a country other than the United States. Responding new members who were born outside the United States represent sixty-eight countries, most commonly Vietnam, Mexico, the Philippines, and Canada (see figure 1.4).

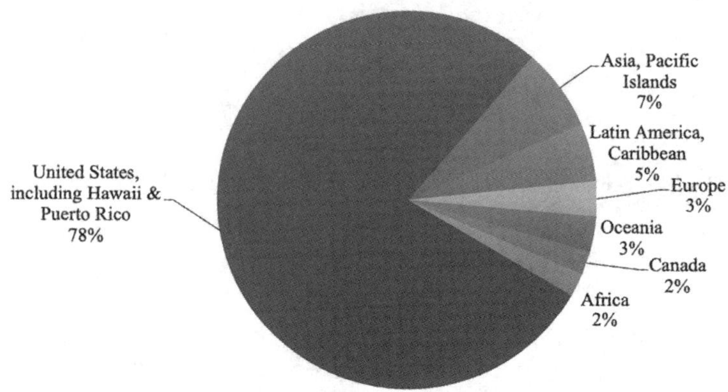

Figure 1.4. Regions of the world where new religious were born. *Source*: Data from Gautier and Do (2020).

On average, those who were born in a country other than the United States first came to live in the United States at age twenty-one. A third arrived as children, aged seventeen or younger. Another third arrived as young adults, between the ages of eighteen and twenty-five. The other third arrived as adults, aged twenty-six or older. This means that, in addition to many cultural differences in their upbringing, many of these new members also are not native English speakers; they reported a total of fifty-nine different languages that they speak. Eight in ten women new members reported English as their first language, but about 5 percent each speak Spanish or Vietnamese as their first language. Among those women who speak Spanish or Vietnamese as their first language, 5 percent speak only that language fluently; 82 percent speak two languages and 13 percent speak three or more fluently.

Family and Faith Background of New Members

As one might expect from the discussion above about nativity of new members, it should come as no surprise to learn that nearly four in ten new members (38%) have at least one parent who was born outside the United States—most typically Mexico, Vietnam, the Philippines, or Canada. Those who had at least one foreign-born parent are more likely to say that they grew up in a family that was among the working poor, but overall about three in four new members had a middle-class background. The bulk of these new members (42%) grew up in the Midwest, although those with at least one foreign-born parent were more likely to have grown up in the Pacific West (the states of California, Oregon, Washington, Hawaii, or Alaska). Nearly all women religious (95%) have siblings. They are usually the eldest or a middle child in a family of three children, on average.

Nearly all of these new members were raised Catholic in a family in which at least one parent was Catholic, as was the case for previous generations of religious. It is not at all uncommon, however, for some of them to have come to the faith as adults, converting on average in their late teens or early twenties, which is typical for other Catholics in general. Other CARA studies of women who enter religious life for the first time[2] show between 76 and 89 percent reported that religion was very important to their mothers and fathers. Around nine in ten report attending Mass together as a family weekly or more often. At least a third had a relative that they knew who was ecclesially connected to the Church, serving as a priest, a deacon, or a religious sister or brother. Thus, four in ten women religious shared that starting a discussion with their family about their vocation was easy for them. Around three in ten report that a family member (most often, their mother or father) spoke to them about religious life. Additionally, nearly all had at least one friend who was a priest, a deacon, or a religious sister or brother who interacted with them while they were contemplating the idea of a religious vocation for themselves.

Half of them attended parish-based Catholic religious education while they were children, and close to half attended a Catholic

---

2. "Women and Men Entering Religious Life: The Entrance Class of . . ." has been published annually by CARA since 2012. See appendix for more detail about this and other CARA studies cited in this book.

elementary or middle school. This was also typical of religious of earlier generations, although the children growing up in the 1950s through the 1970s were more likely to have had religious as teachers and principals in those Catholic schools. These new members were unlikely to have had a Catholic sister as a teacher in their Catholic elementary school. A little more than a tenth of them were homeschooled by a Catholic parent for at least some of their education, on average for about eight years. This is an increasing trend in the United States, particularly among Catholic families who do not have access to Catholic schools and/or are unsatisfied with the schools available to them.

New members were more likely to encounter a Catholic sister in high school or in college, for those who attended a Catholic high school or a Catholic college or university. About four in ten attended a Catholic high school and the same proportion attended a Catholic college or university. These institutions are more likely than Catholic elementary and middle schools to have religious serving as teachers, campus ministers, chaplains, or administrators.

Higher Education and Work Experience of New Members

Another substantial difference between new members of religious institutes today and those who entered religious life in generations before them is the amount of education and experience they bring with them to religious life. As stated earlier, it was more common for women of previous generations to enter a religious institute right out of high school, with no work experience at all. Many of them went on to pursue higher education as a religious, and a number of large religious institutes of women even founded Catholic colleges for women so that they would be able to accommodate the very large numbers of sisters who were working toward a degree while they taught in a Catholic school or worked in a Catholic hospital.

The situation is dramatically different today. Most of those Catholic women's colleges are now closed. Religious institutes are much less likely to subsidize the cost of a sister's education and instead encourage women to attain a college degree while they are considering a vocation to religious life. If a woman accrues educational debt while she is attending college, she must be free of that debt before she can be accepted as a candidate in a religious institute. Therefore, many young women who are considering a vocation go on to spend several years working while they pay off their educational debt. They continue to meet with a vocation director, mentor, or spiritual director while they are working, and most typically enter a religious institute in their mid-to-late twenties.

Therefore, new members in religious life today have completed most or all of their education before they enter their institute. Seven in ten have completed at least one college degree before they enter: about half have a bachelor's degree, 17 percent have earned a master's degree, and another 4 percent have a doctoral degree. Most of these new members (eight in ten) have also worked before they entered. Three in four women worked full time in a job or career before they entered religious life. The amount of work and life experience they bring to religious life is vastly greater than that of the generations before them.

These women also bring a great deal of pastoral ministry experience with them into religious life. In addition to regular Mass attendance and participation in Catholic campus ministry, many of them were involved in a more formal way in some aspect of parish ministry. For example, more than half of these new members participated in a parish youth group, Life Teen, or some other youth ministry group while growing up. More than half had a more formal liturgical role in their parish, serving as a lector or extraordinary minister of the Eucharist, or in some other volunteer ministry in their parish. About four in ten participated in a parish music ministry and about the same percentage participated in campus ministry in their college or university. Four in ten participated in a Bible study or a young adult ministry in their parish.

Beyond the parish, many of these new members have used their faith to evangelize other young people they encounter. A quarter have participated in the Right to Life March, held annually in

Washington, DC, before they entered their institute. Some of them attended the march as teens, and others served as sponsors and chaperones to bring busloads of teens from their home parishes to experience the event. One in five has participated in World Youth Day, which is a global evangelization event featuring a Mass led by the pope and held every other year in various locations around the world. Again, some attended the event as a participant while others served as chaperones for parish and diocesan youth groups. At least one in ten has participated in a Steubenville University High School Youth Conference, either as a high school student participant or as a college student helping to organize and lead the event. Nearly one in ten was involved with the National Catholic Youth Conference, a national event for teens, and about the same percentage was involved with FOCUS, the Fellowship of Catholic University Students. Finally, more than a tenth ministered as a volunteer in a longer-term religious institute volunteer program, such as the Jesuit Volunteer Corps or the Mercy Volunteers, before they entered religious life.

Influences on New Members Discerning a Vocation to Religious Life

Just as the generations before them, new members say that they were attracted to religious life by a sense of call to religious life, a desire for prayer and spiritual growth, and a desire for a deeper relationship with God. Their personal stories of encounter with God are varied and powerful in their descriptions. They show us the depth of soul searching and personally mature faith that these women possess. Said one woman in a focus group:

> *For me it was a desire for community after having been in parish ministry for twenty years as a single person. Everywhere I looked didn't have the fulfillment of community that I was looking for. It's not that there wasn't community . . . but I wanted to work and pray and live with people of the same mindset and heartset, if you will. While I had a great Catholic education, it wasn't*

that—I am an older vocation, as it were—those relationships as a young child and as a high schooler were certainly important, but they weren't the only thing. So, there was an inward nag and it would not go away. And so, it was that nag for community life for a stable place and to just be with people of like mind and heart.

Another related:

Little by little, I came to feel that . . . for me it wouldn't be enough to get married or to live a single life. I needed to give everything. If I was going to give something, I needed to give everything. That was part of the initial attraction. Then I met my community when I was sixteen. Actually, I was not attracted to my mission at the beginning, but I was attracted to the relationship with Jesus that I saw that the members had, their joy. Then also I met a lot of members who entered or began their religious life at a younger age when we used to have a high school. I think that kind of tapped into that desire to give everything, like even youth and the years of my life that I didn't realize I could give to God.

Many new members reflect on their life experiences, primarily in college and in their work, and how those experiences gradually brought them to a realization that God was calling them to religious life. One sister told us:

I was a history major in college. As I studied more about injustices, and I studied abroad in South Africa and experienced a lot of injustices, it really awoke this place in me. I guess I became very conflicted about how I wanted to live and how I want others to live. Basically, it was centered around community, simplicity, social justice, prayer, serve the poor, live close to the poor, and I would just kind of see, "Oh I'm describing what religious life is.". . . . I came back from South Africa more intentional about discerning what I would want to do with my life. I entered pretty young because I felt pretty clear about how I wanted to live my life.

Another sister described how, when she was in college, encouragement of her musical talent gradually brought her to recognize her call from God.

> *When I think of my initial call, I was in college. I hadn't gone to Catholic school for high school or grade school, but we went to church regularly as a family. I was in college when I decided I wanted to play my instrument at Mass. I had an opportunity to practice with another sister who helped me along the way with getting my instrumental playing together for church, which was really cool. It also opened that door and let me see a glimpse of what religious life was like for her in living community. That for me was my initial call to religious life.*

Attraction to a Particular Religious Institute

A vocation to religious life is more than just an idea or a spiritual practice. After all, one can pray and even worship alone, one can study the spiritual masters and become versed in matters of faith without joining a religious institute, one can certainly do all manner of good works without becoming a religious, but one cannot become a religious without entering a particular religious institute. So how do those considering a vocation to religious life find the right religious institute for them? How and where do they seek out and meet with people who have chosen such a vocation? What makes them select one particular institute rather than another?

Not surprisingly, since more than half of these new members are millennials who grew up with a closer familiarity to technology than to religious life, some of them said that they began their search for a religious community online.

> *I did all my research online. I Googled the congregations. I found what was important was their mission and charism statements. I reached out to several, visited several, and noticed that for one in particular, the relationships were easy. They kept inviting and I kept saying yes. You start to feel comfortable and at home. They're still inviting, I'm still saying yes.*

The most common way the new members first became acquainted with their religious institute was in an institution, such as a school, where the members served. For some, it was sisters working in their parish, teaching in their high school, or serving as a campus minister in their college. Four in ten new members said that this was the way they first met religious sisters.

I grew up with my congregation, but I felt it was fair to check out other ones too before I committed to mine. So, I did a little bit of visiting, you know, but for me it was an easy decision. It felt right to me. I made a lay commitment first when I was in college, and we were all going around the circle saying why we wanted to be in this lay community, and all the things that people were saying were what I grew up with. That was my view of the Church and not just of this congregation. So, I said, "Well shoot, I don't want that to end once I graduate from college or whatever and I feel a really strong pull to help that continue in our world." I think that there is a need for our specific charism to exist in the world and I can play a role in helping that continue. Not to say that the lay couldn't, but as a religious, it's just a little more fit to me. Not better, not worse, but to me that is kind of where I came in.

What really helped these new members to make their decision to enter was primarily their experiences of spending time with particular women religious and getting to know them.

For me, I began thinking about religious life most seriously when I was a sophomore in high school. I knew of one sister who was at my high school. I didn't feel comfortable yet talking to her about it, or talking to anyone about it. I just went online to try to find out as much as I could. When I was a senior in high school, the sisters from my community came to visit and have lunch with a few of us. . . . In meeting them, they're real people. I could see myself doing that, and doing that happily. From there I just kept in communication with them, visited them. In visiting with them I saw their spirituality and I saw aspects of their spirituality that made sense for me.

For most, it was a strong identification with one or more role models in a particular community that led them to select their particular institute.

> *After college, I moved out West and taught on the Navaho reservation. I met one of the sisters from our community out there. It was not the spiritual stuff, it was more of the faith through action. She was always doing things like out cutting bushes, mowing grass, doing that kind of stuff, waxing, stripping floors. She'd ask for help. I could help with those things. Those were safe things. I kind of helped with that, cleaning the church, doing those different things. She's like, so, faith and action, you're kind of doing and finding God in those things. Kind of meeting her through doing those non-spiritual things, but those kinds of faith through action is kind of what drew me to community, and kind of where it blossomed from there.*

Another said:

> *I didn't know any religious or sisters growing up until I went to university. As soon as I met the sisters there, it was just something different about them and something that called me to see myself with them. They had a lot of joy, and they really were always present on campus.*

When asked about various factors that may have attracted them to their religious institute, most said that it was the spirituality and the charism of the institute that most attracted them to their particular religious institute. At least seven in ten new members say these aspects attracted them very much.

> *What attracted me first to my community was their joy. That was the thing, I'm like "That could be me." The first order that I was looking into . . . their charism, their mission wasn't something I thought that I could do. The order that I joined, this is exactly what I want to do. This is exactly my fix. Honestly, since entering and since being received and everything I feel whole for the first time in my life.*

Other things that at least three in four new members said very much influenced their decision to enter their particular institute included the prayer life, the community life, and the way the Gospel values were lived out in the institute.

Encouragement and Support for Religious Life

Entering a religious institute is a counter-cultural act. It requires a certain level of maturity and self-knowledge to deliberately commit one's life to poverty, chastity, and obedience in a group dedicated to community, prayer, and ministry. These new members do not take this decision lightly, nor do they commit to this lifestyle without support from others. We asked new members about the amount of encouragement they received from different people when they were first considering entering their religious institute. More than six in ten said that they received "very much" support for their decision from the other members of their religious institute, from their vocation director or team, and from their spiritual director. Half said that they received as much support from other men and women religious with whom they are acquainted. About four in ten indicated that they received "very much" support from diocesan priests, deacons, or bishops. These people all have firsthand experience with the lifestyle and would be expected to be supportive of those who are considering such a commitment.

Others, who may not have such firsthand experience of religious life, appear to be somewhat less encouraging of a vocation to religious life. Friends, parishioners, teachers, youth/campus ministers, coworkers all are at least somewhat encouraging of a vocation to religious life, but these women indicate that only around a third of these groups provided "very much" encouragement to them for this decision. This reflects the counter-cultural nature of a religious vocation in our very secular and individualistic society. In a focus group that was reflecting on the greatest obstacles to vocational discernment, one new member said this:

> *An unsupportive culture, especially familial or local church community. A widespread lack of understanding of the religious vocation among diocesan clergy (and bishops).*

Said another, reflecting her lack of familiarity with religious institutes at the time she was discerning:

> *For women religious, [the greatest obstacle is] the lack of support/ education at the parish level. I had no idea how to even begin discerning after I realized that was what I was being called to do! It made it a rather bumpy ride, but ended up well.*

Perhaps most discouraging, parents, siblings, and other family members seem to be among the least supportive of a religious vocation, according to these new members. Just three in ten or fewer reported receiving "very much" encouragement from parents, siblings, grandparents, or other family members. In focus groups, these new members spoke of a lack of support from family members as being particularly difficult for them. Said one:

> *I think one of the greatest obstacles today is a lack of support from family members and friends. Vocations and vows are a real mystery to people and therefore many are scared to either accept their vocation or those of others dear to them, as if they're "throwing their life away" in answering a call.*

Another, reflecting a bit more generally about lack of support from family and friends, mentioned how difficult this resistance became for her when she was trying to pay down her student debt so that she could enter her chosen religious institute:

> *I perceive that in the United States, entering religious life has many obstacles. Aside from being counter-cultural, my biggest obstacle was lack of parental support and my student loans. . . . What shocked me was encountering priests who did not believe in me or God's ability to provide for the seemingly impossible, which was discouraging.*

Fortunately, some of this resistance appears to abate as family and friends experience firsthand the joy and peace of mind that comes with religious life. When new members were asked to evaluate the level of encouragement and support they receive from family members now that they have made their decision to enter religious life, more than seven in ten indicate that the level of support has increased (see figure 1.5).

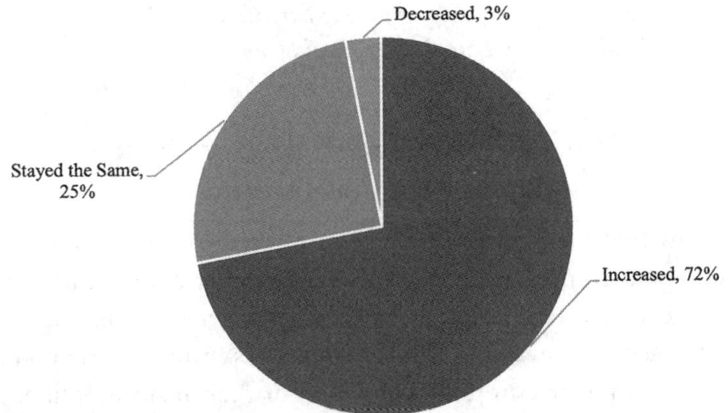

Figure 1.5. Familial support after entering religious life. *Source*: Data from Gautier and Do (2020).

Several new members described in focus groups how the initial resistance from their family members had subsided over time, as they grew more familiar with religious life and what it entails:

> *I don't think my dad was very convinced actually until my first profession—we had recreation with all the sisters that night and one of the things available was ping pong, so he and my now brother-in-law and my sister and I were all playing ping pong and I think my dad was caught off guard by how competitive some of the sisters are, but in a good way. For him to be able to see like "Oh my goodness they are normal," because he was always supportive of me but didn't really get the whole thing.*

> *I think with my family, for four years they were waiting for me to come back. "You're not going to persevere." I didn't do it for them. I did it because I believe there is something in religious life that is giving me meaning. I have peace.*
>
> *And I remember once when my parents came to visit when I was in the novitiate and the novice directress told my mom—they were talking—my family is not Catholic so my vocation has been hard for them, but she told my mom, "She's free to leave anytime," and that was really helpful for my parents and I think I just realized like wow I am, I have always been free.*

What New Members Like Best about Their Religious Institute

Now that they have made a commitment to this lifestyle and have spent some time living with a particular community, new members have a lot to say about their experience of religious life. When asked to evaluate their religious institute, new members were most positive in their evaluation of their institute's fidelity to the Church and its teachings as well as in the care and support their institute provides to its elderly members. More than three in four new members report that their institute is excellent in these two aspects. In focus groups, some of the women mentioned these aspects when asked what they liked most about being a member of their religious institute. Said one new member:

> *So, we say in our constitutions that we are a community for mission. And we are. And I think that's what it is, so that the ninety-five-year-old sister who's in the infirmary is community for mission. The sister who's studying to become a psychiatric nurse for the homeless is community for mission. It's that charism in community that's an inspiration and the joy of the sisters.*

Another described a ninety-three-year-old sister in her community and what an inspiration she has been to others in the institute:

They do everything with the complete depth that they have, no matter what their ministry is. We recently just had a sister go to the nursing home across the street. She was ninety-three, still doing the whole dining room. She's done many things. She founded a spirituality center for our community. She's done so many things, she's been superior of our mother house. She did so many wonderful things for our community. She did the dining room just with as much fervor as she did everything else. It's just her heart and her spirituality and her joy for Christ and her vocation. I could never imagine myself not wanting to do that. It's just so much joy in her life. If I'm like half the person she is at ninety-three, I just hope that that's my future. Really seeing the sisters before us and standing on their shoulders and saying yes, this is what I want to be, this is who I am. In Christ's eyes, I can do this, too. I think that's for sure something that gives me hope for my future.

Following on that, another sister said:

Yeah, every single time I have troubles and challenges, I somehow find myself looking at the sister's ring. It gives me hope, such fidelity, in any age that they're at. So much like it flows from their union with God and their eucharistic lifestyle. I said, "I want to be like that, too, that fidelity that they're witnessing." Now, recently the juniors were able to see the archives and have a conversation with our deceased sisters in knowing their stories. It's different now when we visit them in their tombs, and just seeing what their life story is in the fidelity up to the end. That gives me so much hope, despite all the challenges there are.

Another new member described her institute in these words:

I would say it's the Eucharist that sustains me. When I was in seventh grade, my computer teacher organized a kind of a eucharistic adoration group for the kids. It was in that time that my eyes were really opened to see, "Oh my gosh, religion is more than just what you read in the textbook. It's this person who loves me and who I love, too." Then, when I first went to visit the sisters, I saw on the outside of their chapel the words, "The Blessed Sacrament is my life, my bliss. To this I owe the grace of my own vocation." When I read that, it gave me goose bumps. It's just so beautiful! When I start getting confused, and start thinking about the negatives, and worry about the future of our community, it always comes down to the Eucharist. How our founder really was so in love with the Blessed Sacrament, that I want for my life to have that particular emphasis.

Two in three are equally positive about the sense of identity among members of their religious institute and the welcome and support it provides to new members. The same proportion evaluate the communal prayer experiences of their institute as excellent. Said one new member in a focus group:

It's being with other people who want to place God at the very center of their lives. That's not weird, or different. That's what they want to do with their life. Knowing that they're there to support me, and they're there in my hard times and they're there to celebrate the joyful pieces of my life as well, I think that's one of the greatest gifts of community. . . . I live now with one sister who is in leadership. I have obviously known her before she was in leadership. Even our community minister now, I knew her before she took on that role. Before I entered I would have thought, the community minister, she's so high, above everybody else, but they're not. They're servant leaders. Yes, the authority is with them. I do give them my obedience certainly. They're just like the rest of us. They're servant leaders. I just appreciate that so much.

In another focus group, a new member had this to say about her institute:

What sustains me are three things. First and foremost is the Eucharist. We have eucharistic adoration every day and daily Mass. And I feel like if I didn't have that, I wouldn't be able to bring God's love in the same way. So, the second thing would be the mission, teaching. I love being with the children. And the third is community. Those three things go hand in hand, not just living in the same house, but really community. That experience of sharing life together and doing fun things together, praying together, like really having a strong community life.

In fact, out of twenty different aspects of religious life on which new members were asked to evaluate their institute, only two aspects received an excellent rating by fewer than four in ten new members. According to these new members, work remains to be done in their institutes around the topics of diversity of cultures within the institute and communal work around racism. Although half or more say that their institute is at least good in these two aspects, just one in five rates her institute as excellent in either aspect. In elaborating on what remains to be done in their religious institutes in each of these aspects, new members wrote in these comments about their hopes for the future:

An increased ability to serve the Hispanic communities in our Church.

Embracing our diversity more effectively, consolidating our Regions in fewer places of great need in the world, educating formally more members, affirming community life, training younger members of color to take leadership roles, remaining in dialogue with the Church, embracing ministries that meet urgent/ongoing needs of the marginalized.

Going globally to Asia, especially to Vietnam.

More cultural diversity and openness to new ways of expressing charism in different cultural contexts.

More members from diverse cultures and foundations in other countries. A more organic structure that allows us to be more about mission. For our community's intercultural work to serve as a blueprint for other congregations.

> *More women entering (especially from diverse cultures, socio-economic backgrounds, and ministerial backgrounds).*

> *Originally, my community was formed for the US-born vocations. After ten years, I would like to see how we embrace other nationalities.*

> *Thriving, with increased vocations, even greater cultural and ethnic diversity, continued diversity of ministries, and increased communication and collaboration with other religious institutions, hopefully being known for preaching the truth, and upholding the truth and human rights.*

> *We do the internal work on racism as a community. We embrace cultural diversity and not only talk about it.*

Summary and Conclusion

As noted at the beginning of this chapter, women entering religious life today are quite different from those entering a few generations ago, and the religious institutes they are entering have also changed dramatically in the past fifty or sixty years. These women are older, more educated, more experienced, and many have a more clear-eyed appreciation for the counter-cultural action they take by professing vows in religious life. The institutes they enter today are typically smaller and composed of a larger proportion of elderly members than those of the 1950s and 1960s.

In other ways, though, these women are remarkably similar to those of previous generations. They possess a strong faith, sense of purpose, and desire to make a difference in the world by living in prayer and community with others who share their faith and commitment. They profess the same lifelong vows of poverty, chastity, and obedience that have been a hallmark of religious life for centuries. They make a difference in the world by the lives they live together. The religious institutes they enter are also, in many ways, very consistent with religious institutes of previous generations in that they follow the same canonical guidelines that have always controlled religious life. Though the demographics and outward appearances change, the essential character of religious life really has not changed. Women continue to be drawn to a fuller expression of commitment to God through living out religious vows.

In the next chapter we explore in depth one of the more interesting changes to religious life in recent decades—the increased cultural diversity of religious life and among religious institutes in the United States.

*Thu T. Do and
Jonathon L. Wiggins*

CHAPTER 2

Cultural Diversity in Vocations to Religious Life in the United States

In the last few decades, the Catholic Church in the United States has been experiencing an increase in cultural and ethnic diversity among its Catholic population. According to the 2018 General Social Survey, 58 percent of adult Catholic respondents self-identified as non-Hispanic White and just more than a third identified as Hispanic or Latino (35%). Five percent self-identified as non-Hispanic Black, African American, African, or Afro-Caribbean. Few Catholics self-identified as an "other" (see figure 2.1) race or ethnicity, with respondents writing in mainly that they are Asian, Native Hawaiian or Pacific Islander, American Indian or Alaskan Native Catholics.

CARA estimated total population sizes for these racial and ethnic groups by aggregating the data within the boundaries of US Catholic dioceses, resulting in the thirteen different subgroups as shown in table 2.1, which estimates the Catholic affiliation percentage and estimated Catholic population totals for each of these groups.

In 2013, CARA identified a total of 6,332 parishes that are known to serve a particular racial, ethnic, cultural, and/or linguistic community (36% of all US parishes). Some parishes served two or more ethnic groups. Accordingly, a total of 6,570 communities were identified (see figure 2.2).

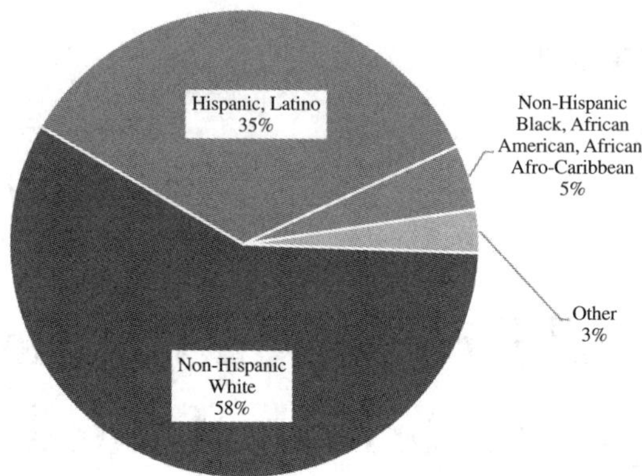

Figure 2.1. US Catholics by race and ethnicity. *Source*: Data from General Social Survey (Chicago: National Opinion Research Center, University of Chicago, 2018).

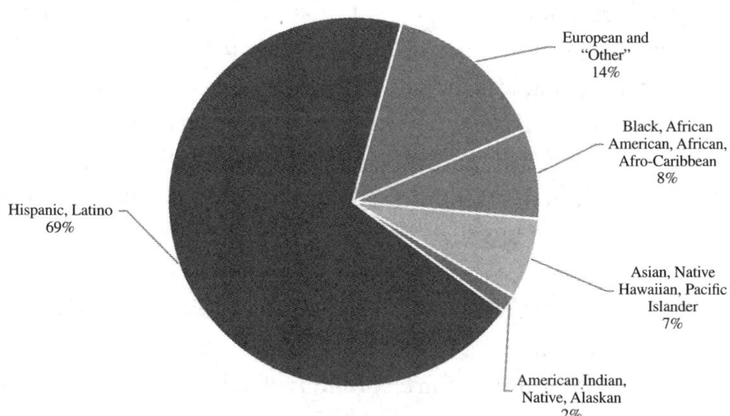

Figure 2.2. US parishes known to serve specific racial, ethnic, cultural, or linguistic communities, 2013. *Source*: Data from Mark M. Gray, Mary L. Gautier, and Thomas P. Gaunt, *Cultural Diversity in the Catholic Church in the United States* (Washington, DC: Center for Applied Research in the Apostolate, 2014).

	Catholic Population	Catholic Affiliation (%)	Share of Catholic population (%)
White (non-Hispanic)	39,357,880	20.0	51.5
Hispanic or Latino	28,426,421	47.0	37.2
Born in the United States	*15,208,135*	*45.6*	*20.3*
Foreign-born	*13,218,286*	*51.2*	*17.6*
Asian	3,402,029	18.5	4.4
Vietnamese	*515,047*	*27.8*	*0.7*
Filipino	*268,345*	*7.2*	*0.4*
Chinese	*313,579*	*7.2*	*0.4*
Korean	*144,544*	*10.0*	*0.2*
Indian	*268,345*	*6.4*	*0.4*
Black, African American, African, Afro-Caribbean (Non-Hispanic)	3,085,299	7.6	4.0
American Indian, Alaska Native	653,123	28.4	0.9
Native Hawaiian, Pacific Islander	16,705	27.3	0.02
Total	74,941,457	22.8	100

Table 2.1. US Catholic population, by race and ethnicity, 2019. *Sources*: Data from American Community Survey, General Social Survey, Gallup, Pew Research Center.

Among those 6,570 parishes, the largest proportion of these parishes (69%) serve Hispanic or Latino Catholic communities. The next largest proportion (14%) serves European Catholic communities (such as Italian, Polish, or Ukrainian Catholics); followed by 8 percent serving Black, African American, African, or Afro-Caribbean Catholics; 7 percent serving Asian, Native Hawaiian, or Pacific Islander Catholics; and 2 percent serving American Indian or Alaskan Native Catholics.

As the United States has become more racially and ethnically diverse, so has religious life. In 2020, commissioned by the Conrad N. Hilton Foundation, CARA conducted a study to explore the impact of increasing cultural diversity on religious life in the United States.[1] A total of 618 women religious who entered religious life in US religious institutes since 2003 participated in the study. Among these women religious, three-fourths (75%) identify as Caucasian, followed by Asian (11%), Hispanic (10%), Black (2%), and other ethnicities (2%) (see figure 2.3). As mentioned in the previous chapter, research has shown a consistent percentage of women religious entering religious life in the last fifteen years in each category of racial or ethnic background.

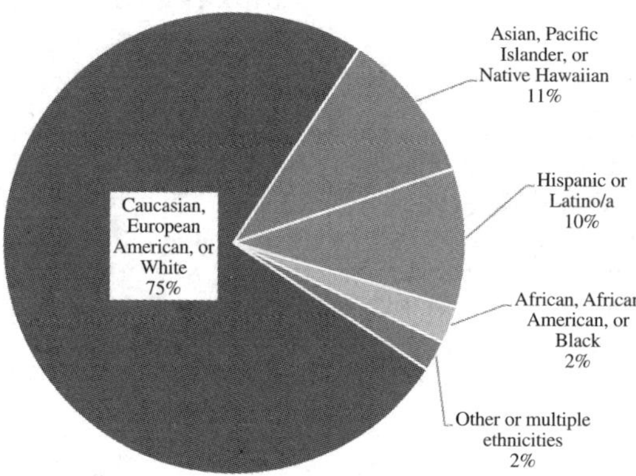

Figure 2.3. Cultural and ethnic backgrounds of US women religious. *Source:* Data from Thu Do, Jonathon Wiggins, and Thomas Gaunt, *Cultural Diversity in Vocations to Religious Life in the United States: A National Study of New Religious Members* (Washington, DC: Center for Applied Research in the Apostolate, 2021).

Moreover, contemporary women religious are increasingly immigrants or the children or grandchildren of immigrants from Catholic countries outside of Europe, especially Asia, Latin America, and

1. See appendix at the end for a more detailed description of this and other CARA studies used in this book.

Africa. The same study shows one in five new women religious was born in a country other than in the United States (21%). Black sisters (87%) are most likely to be foreign-born, followed by Asians (75%), Hispanics (43%), and Whites (8%). One woman religious, who had lived within her religious institute in communities in the United States as well as in other countries, wrote this regarding her hopes for the future of her institute:

> *I am a part of an international, multicultural community. From my experience in this country, we celebrate this diversity and strive to integrate our different prayer groups who speak different languages and have different cultural backgrounds with one another. Having also experienced my community charism outside my native culture in other countries, my hope is that we continue to learn how to grow in the area of multicultural community life. I pray we continue learning how we can enter other cultures and how we can receive missionaries from other cultures. These discussions already exist, but I believe we can go deeper.*[2]

Noticeable in her observation is that cultural diversity is recognized among religious members as both a blessing and a challenge. From these cultural and ethnic perspectives, this chapter examines what impact parishes and family life have had on women religious' vocational discernment before entering religious life, what their experiences of cultural diversity within their religious institutes have been, and what challenges such diversity poses to these women religious.

Family Factors Affecting Vocational Discernment

Part of understanding how one's family affects discernment of a vocation to religious life is knowing and understanding the ethnic or cultural backgrounds of the families. Also influential is

2. Mary L. Gautier and Thu T. Do, *Recent Vocations to Religious Life: A Report for the National Religious Vocation Conference*, A CARA report (Washington, DC: Center for Applied Research in the Apostolate, 2020), 138.

what country the person was born in and/or how many genera-tions ago they or their families immigrated to the United States. Seven in ten (70%) of the women religious surveyed in the 2021 study were born in the United States of US-born parents (third generation or later), one in ten (9%) has one or two parents who immigrated to the United States (second generation), and about two in ten (21%) immigrated to the United States themselves (first generation). (See figure 2.4.)

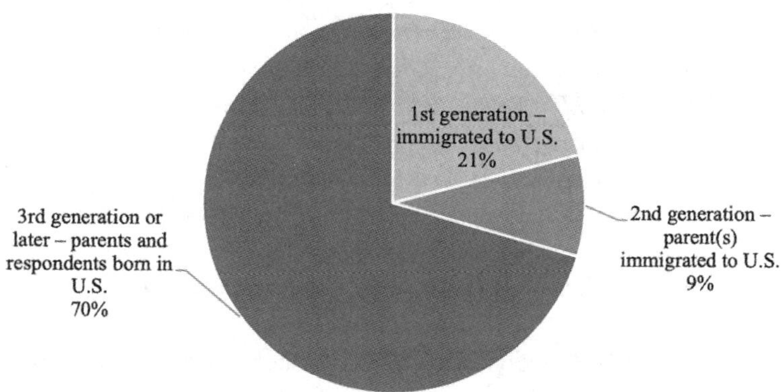

Figure 2.4. Generations of immigration. *Source*: Data from Do, Wiggins, and Gaunt (2021).

Comparing different ethnicities according to their generation of immigration, Black (87%) and Asian (75%) women religious in the survey are most likely to be first generation, with White women religious (88%) most likely to be third generation. (See figure 2.5.) Hispanics are split among three generations, with four in ten of them of the first generation (43%).

As CARA research consistently shows,[3] various family prac-tices are influential in religious members' vocational discernment.

---

3. Patricia Wittberg, "The Influences of Families on Religious Vocations," in *Pathways to Religious Life*, ed. Thomas Gaunt (New York: Oxford University Press, 2018), 37–59.

Two in three (68%) women religious say that their families had "some" or "a great" impact on their vocational discernment. The younger the respondent, the more likely her family had an impact. More than half (53%) of early Millennials (ages twenty-eight and younger), for example, say that their family had "a great" impact on their vocational discernment, compared to 37 percent of late Millennials (ages twenty-nine to thirty-eight), 30 percent of those of the Post–Vatican II Generation (ages thirty-nine to fifty-nine), and 13 percent of those of the Vatican II Generation (ages sixty and older).

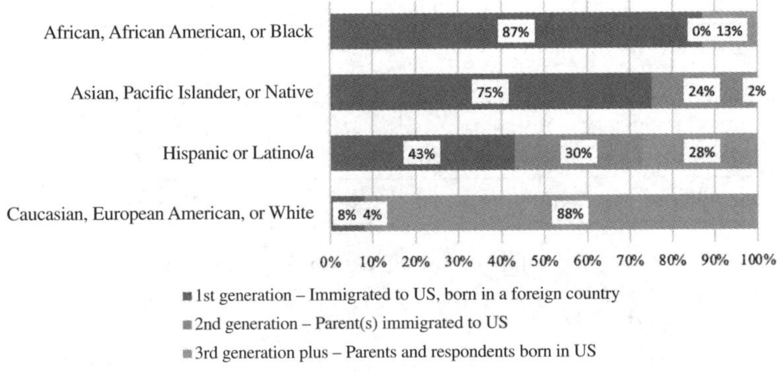

Figure 2.5. Generation when family immigrated to the United States. *Source*: Data from Do, Wiggins, and Gaunt (2021).

The recent survey also shows differences depending on when one or one's family immigrated to the United States. It asked women religious about various religious and family practices in their families, shown in table 2.2, which presents those factors that had "a great" impact overall, as well as generation of immigration.

	All %	First Generation %	Second Generation %	Third or Later Generation %
Attending Masses or other religious services as a family	64	66	63	63
Getting to know a priest or a religious brother or sister/nun besides family members	57	53	60	58
My parents instilling in me a prayer life	53	64	58	50
Active participation in parish life as family	50	57	51	48
Sense of religiosity in my family	46	49	57	44
Daily prayers as a family	41	50	45	37

Table 2.2. Family-related factors having "a great" impact on respondents' vocational discernment before entering religious life. *Source*: Data from Do, Wiggins, and Gaunt (2021).

Half to two-thirds of women religious, regardless of generation, identify these four factors as having had "a great" impact on their vocational discernment: attending Masses or other religious services as a family (64%), getting to know a priest or a religious brother or sister/nun besides family members (57%), their parents instilling in them a prayer life (53%), and active participation in parish life as a family (50%). Figure 2.6 shows the factors with the greatest differences by generation of immigration. Prayer-related family factors are especially salient among first-generation respondents, with at least half saying their parents instilling a prayer life in them (64%) and daily prayer as a family (50%) had "a great" impact. Third or later generations are least likely to have reported any of the factors in the figure as having had "a great" impact.

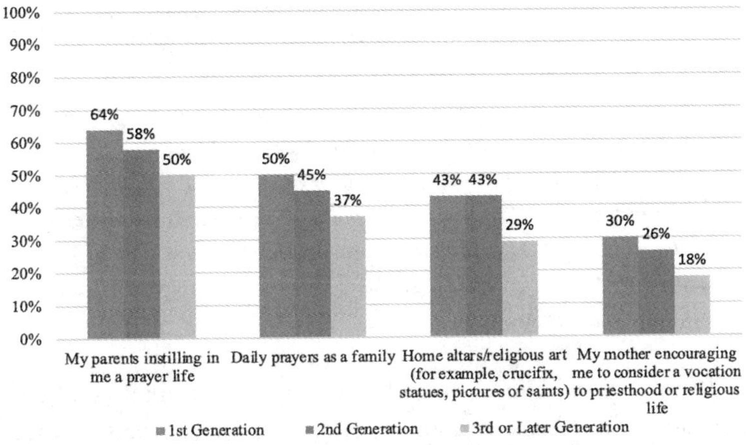

Figure 2.6. Factors that impact respondents' vocational discernment before entering religious life, by immigration generation. *Source*: Data from Do, Wiggins, and Gaunt (2021).

When asked to briefly identify the aspects of the family life that had the most impact on their vocational discernment, women religious shared these in their own words:

> *My mom instilled a prayer life in me with daily family prayer and daily Mass as a family. My dad read the Bible many times and named me after a biblical figure in the Old Testament. My dad instilled the importance of the crucifix in me when I was dating. My older sister encouraged my discernment and I feel safe sharing with her my discernment process. Going to Marian Days in 2013 as a family was the beginning of my vocation discernment.* [First-generation sister from Vietnam.]

> *The fostering of the gift of faith and love for the Church which came from my mother and the maternal side of my family I would say had a great impact on my vocational discernment in the sense that my faith was rooted in and stemmed from my family.* [Second-generation Hispanic sister whose parents emigrated from Ecuador and Mexico.]

> *My mother prayed with me every night when I was little, and took my sister and me to eucharistic adoration often. In this way I learned to trust God, from the little things to the big things. I was consecrated to Mary with my sister when I was young, and when I was a little older there was this particular statue of Our Blessed Mother toward the center of our house that, I think, reminded me of that and always pointed my mind to the higher things. Through Mary and a growing trust in the Lord, I grew in desiring to just give my life to God.* [Third- or later-generation Caucasian sister.]

This study also shows that women religious from different cultural and ethnic backgrounds experience different levels of influences from family and religious practices in their family life on their vocational discernment. Women religious of African/Black, Asian/Pacific Islander, and Hispanic backgrounds are more likely than those of Caucasian/European backgrounds to find that their family members' vocation promotion, such as encouragement and witnessing siblings or relatives as religious or priests, strongly impacted their vocational discernment. They are also most likely to be influenced strongly in their vocational discernment by the religious activities of their family, including performing charitable services and having altars in their homes (see figure 2.7).

Parish Factors Affecting Vocational Discernment

Besides the impact of the family environment on religious vocational discernment, parish life experiences can also nourish religious vocations. Data show that a combined 83 percent say that a parish had "some" (38%) or "a great" (44%) impact on their vocational discernment, which is 14 percentage points greater than the reported impact their families had on their discernment (68% for impacts from family).

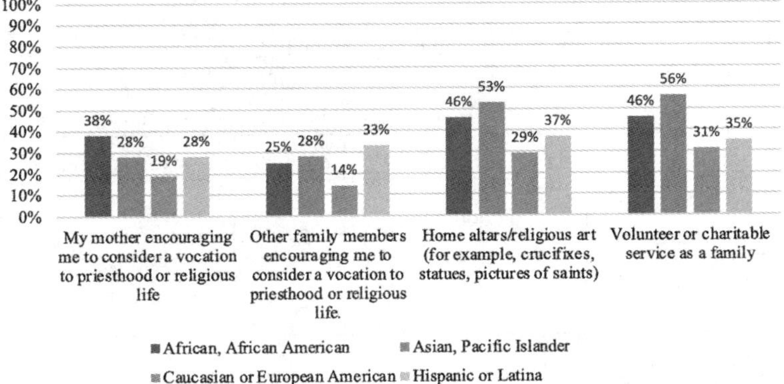

Figure 2.7. Factors that impact respondents' vocational discernment before entering religious life, by ethnic background. *Source*: Data from Do, Wiggins, and Gaunt (2021).

In the survey for this 2021 study, women religious were asked to share the city and country of the parish that had the greatest impact on their vocational discernment. Their age when they encountered that parish as well as whether that parish was in the United States (88%) or elsewhere (12%) varies by the cultural and ethnic background of the respondents. Generally, non-White sisters (33%) are more likely than White sisters (5%) to have identified a parish in a foreign country. As can be seen in table 2.3 below, among those reporting that the parish with the greatest impact on their vocation was a US-based parish, they were most likely to have been influenced by this parish as adults. In contrast, among those whose influential parish was in another country, non-White respondents are more likely to report that they attended it before they reached age eighteen. Asian respondents were especially likely (55%) to report doing so.

	All	African, African American	Asian, Pacific Islander	Caucasian or European American	Hispanic or Latina
US Parish	*(N = 498)*	*(N = 4)*	*(N = 40)*	*(N = 412)*	*(N = 42)*
High school age or younger	24%	0%	27%	24%	21%
Ages 18 and above	46%	100%	58%	45%	48%
Both of the above	30%	0%	15%	31%	31%
Foreign Parish	*(N = 65)*	*(N = 10)*	*(N = 20)*	*(N = 23)*	*(N = 12)*
High school age or younger	35%	40%	55%	17%	33%
Ages 18 and above	37%	30%	30%	48%	33%
Both of the above	28%	30%	15%	35%	34%

Table 2.3. Influential parish's location and the age levels when respondents attended it. *Source*: Data from Do, Wiggins, and Gaunt (2021).

The ten parish characteristics listed in table 2.4 are those that a third or more of responding religious say had "a great" impact on their discernment of a vocation to religious life. Summarizing the factors, they relate to encouragement and support from parish leaders and parishioners to participation in regular parish activities. Generally, those who identified a foreign parish are more likely than those identifying a US parish to list each factor as having had "a great" impact. Also noteworthy, each of the three factors in table 2.4 that specifically mentions ethnicity (i.e., ethnic Catholic traditions, language Masses are celebrated in, and devotion to an ethnic saint) have much higher percentages among those who identified a foreign parish than those who identified a US parish. Thus, the location of the parish has a correlation with how much impact each factor had on vocational discernment.

	All (N = 618) %	US Parishes (N = 524) %	Foreign Parishes (N =71) %
Masses and liturgies at the parish	66	65	69
Clergy at my parish supporting and encouraging me to discern my religious vocation	49	49	56
Participating in the liturgical ministry at the parish (e.g., lector, extraordinary minister, music)	46	44	62
Individual parishioners supporting and encouraging me to discern my religious vocation	44	43	52
Conversations with priests or religious brothers or sisters at the parish	42	42	49
Overall support and encouragement from the parish	41	39	52
Witnessing the presence of religious sisters, or brothers, or priests in the parish	41	40	48
Masses and liturgies in the language of my ethnic/cultural heritage at the parish	36	32	64
Prayer groups at this parish	35	34	42
Service opportunities	35	33	51
Celebrating ethnic Catholic traditions at this parish	25	21	51
Devotion to a saint of my ethnicity/culture at the parish	18	15	36

Table 2.4. Influential parish-related factors that had "a great" impact on respondents' vocational discernment, by parish type. *Source*: Data from Do, Wiggins, and Gaunt (2021).

Among the same factors that at least a third of respondents overall rated as having "a great" impact on their religious vocational discernment, women religious of African and Asian background are more likely than Caucasian women religious to say these factors have "a great" impact on their vocational discernment (table 2.5). Hispanic/Latina and Asian women religious are most likely to assign "a great" impact to individual parishioners supporting and encouraging them to discern a religious vocation and to having conversations with priests or religious sisters and brothers at the parish, with Caucasian or European American women religious generally less likely to say that these factors had "a great" impact.

In response to an open-ended question about what aspect of their parish had the most impact on their vocational discernment, women religious from both US parishes and from foreign parishes describe their experiences below.

The aspects of this parish that had the most impact on my vocational discernment were the presence of a religious sister, who functioned as my spiritual director for a little over a year, and the individual parishioners who became my close friends and encouraged me regularly to persevere in my discernment. [Second-generation woman religious who is Asian and attended an influential US parish as an adult.]

Participating in the liturgy as an altar server, as a cantor, and as a member of the choir had a great impact. The training I received for these areas allowed me to delve deeper into my faith and understanding of the Mass and the Eucharist. The times of adoration and the Stations of the Cross also greatly impacted my prayer life. [Third-generation woman religious who is Caucasian and attended an influential US parish both as a child and as an adult.]

Opportunities to be involved in meaningful ways in the life of the parish—liturgical ministries, retreat leadership, pastoral council, etc. Also, the joyful witness of our pastor and associate pastor, our pastoral staff and the occasional visits by members of religious congregations. [Third-generation woman religious who is Black/African American and attended an influential US parish as an adult.]

I studied in a Catholic school attached to a parish where I belong. As part of the school program, we had Mass and devotion to the Blessed Mother in church and religious sisters are present. Religion subject is also offered. [First-generation woman religious

	All (N=618) %	African, African American (N=16) %	Asian, Pacific Islander (N=67) %	Caucasian or European American (N=456) %	Hispanic or Latina (N=61) %
Masses and liturgies at the parish	66	71	70	66	62
Clergy at my parish supporting and encouraging me to discern my religious vocation	49	67	51	49	45
Participating in the liturgical ministry at the parish (e.g., lector, extraordinary minister, music)	46	71	61	40	63
Individual parishioners supporting and encouraging me to discern my religious vocation	44	46	51	42	53
Conversations with priests or religious brothers or sisters at the parish	42	43	49	40	55
Overall support and encouragement from the parish	41	57	44	40	43
Witnessing the presence of religious sisters, or brothers, or priests in the parish	41	43	48	39	47
Masses and liturgies in the language of my ethnic/cultural heritage at the parish	36	55	52	32	37
Prayer groups at this parish	35	67	57	30	42
Service opportunities	35	54	54	29	52
Celebrating ethnic Catholic traditions at this parish	25	55	51	17	32
Devotion to a saint of my ethnicity/culture at the parish	18	33	41	11	23

Table 2.5. Influential parish-related factors that had "a great" impact on respondents' vocational discernment, by respondents' ethnicity.
Source: Data from Do, Wiggins, and Gaunt (2021).

who is an immigrant from an Asian country and who attended an influential foreign parish as an adult.]

In my parish we had a vocation group that encourages vocations to priesthood, brotherhood and religious vocations. We visited convents and seminary houses. This helped me to build up my faith and the desire to seek out what my real vocation is. I got myself in the dream. [First-generation woman religious who is an immigrant from an African country and who attended an influential foreign parish as an adult.]

Religious Institute's Openness to Cultural Diversity

Community in religious life is made up of various living situations. Respondents were asked to describe the ethnic makeup of the community where they currently live. Figure 2.8 shows that nine in ten live in a community either with at least one member from her own cultural/ethnic background (43%) or with members from many different cultural/ethnic backgrounds (32%). Just one in ten lives in a community where she is the only one of her cultural/ethnic background (10%). As discussed later in this chapter, these living situations affect their experience of cultural diversity in their religious institutes.

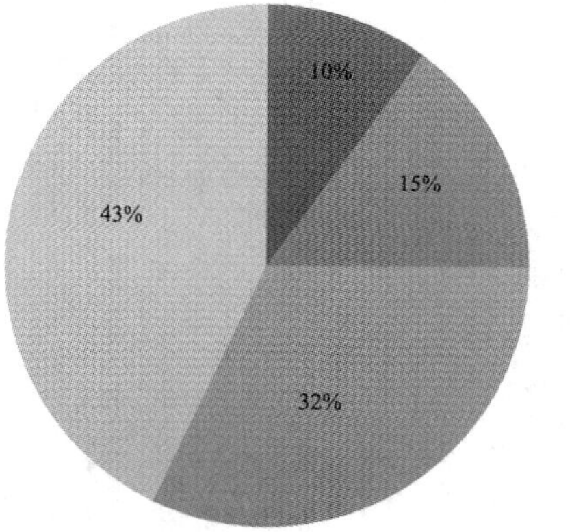

Figure 2.8. Current living situation among women religious. *Source*: Data from Do, Wiggins, and Gaunt (2021).

White women religious are most likely to live in a community with at least one other member of their ethnicity and are least likely to live in a community where they are the only members of their ethnicity. Women religious of other racial or ethnic backgrounds are more likely to live in a community with many cultures or in one where they are the only members of their ethnicity (see figure 2.9).

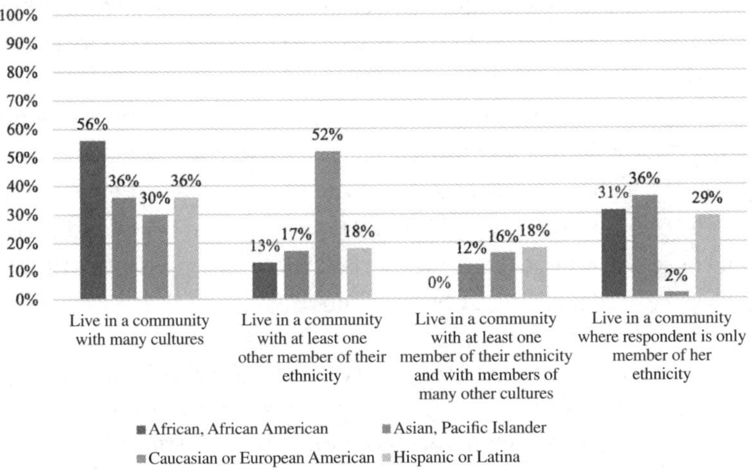

Figure 2.9. Current living situation, by ethnic background. *Source*: Data from Do, Wiggins, and Gaunt (2021).

These current living situations likely result in women religious having different experiences in their religious institutes. Religious institutes with members from various cultural or ethnic backgrounds might be more open to different avenues in which to integrate cultural and ethnic experiences in different aspects of their community life. Table 2.6 displays the aspects of religious life in which respondents are most likely to say their religious institute is "very" open. The table presents the findings for respondents overall as well as by whether a respondent lives with at least one other member of her community that shares her ethnic/

racial background. As is evident in the table, those who are the only members of their ethnicity/race in the community in which they live are significantly less likely than others to say that their community is "very" open to encouraging members to share their culture in community life (56%), to openly discussing cultural differences (51%), to celebrating the feast day of the patron saint of another country or culture (48%), to educating community members about another culture (46%), to encouraging members to learn another language (44%), to integrating foods from other cultures into the community's meals (41%), or to celebrating the holidays of different cultures (40%).

Women religious were also invited to write comments about what their religious institute could do to better accommodate new members from different cultures. The four responses below come from those living in two different types of community and focus on those with suggestions rather than those saying their institutes are already succeeding at being open.

> *Encourage open and honest conversation with members from different cultures. Some of the newer members feel unheard or misunderstood many times.* [Second-generation Asian woman religious who lives in a community with at least one other member of her ethnic background.]

> *Create opportunities to share about our different cultures, strengths and weaknesses of both. Interest in learning more about them, their backgrounds. Find a mentor from same or similar culture to orient and guide them in the initial period of time.* [First-generation African woman religious who lives in a community in which she is the only member of her ethnicity.]

> *Formators and superiors should have an understanding of the cultural background of the sisters under them. When possible, a formandi should at least have a sister to dialogue with from her own background. Some kind of practical workshop or classes*

	All* (N=618) %	Community with at least one other member of respondents' ethnicity (N=474) %	Community where respondent only member of respondents' ethnicity (N=55) %
Accommodating family visit(s) for those whose families live in another country	78	78	78
Welcoming those in initial formation who are from cultures different from the dominant ethnic/racial group of the institute	72	73	67
Encouraging members to share their culture in community life	70	71	56
Celebrating the feast day of the patron saint of another country or culture	69	71	48
Recruiting candidates from cultures different from the dominant ethnic/racial group of the institute	68	68	64
Integrating foods from other cultures into the community's meals	65	67	41
Openly discussing cultural differences	60	61	51
Educating community members about another culture	59	61	46
Encouraging members to learn another language	58	59	44
Celebrating the holidays of different cultures	52	54	40

*"All" includes those who did not respond to the question about their living situation

Table 2.6. Respondents report their religious institute is "very" open in this way. *Source*: Data from Do, Wiggins, and Gaunt (2021).

would be helpful for sisters to learn about the cultures of sisters in their community, and how to best understand the different tendencies in communication, expectations, etc. There should be some accommodation for those sisters from communities with very strong family ties in regards to home visits, etc. Also, it seems that the format of our chapter discussions favors the American style of communication. Maybe the sisters from different countries could be helped to express themselves as delegates. [Second-generation Asian woman religious who lives in a community with at least one other member of her ethnic background.]

There are unintentional blind spots that keep the language where a "minority" is spoken of as "other" and while they are very open and loving and hospitable, this language seeps out. Since it is coming from blind spots, there has not been open dialogue about it because otherwise we think we are already accommodating and inclusive. The challenge is to actually view inter-culturality with a different lens. [Third-generation Hispanic woman religious who lives in a community in which she is the only member of her ethnicity.]

Cultural Challenges of Women Religious within Their Religious Institute

Women religious certainly experience various challenges as vowed members in religious life. Table 2.7 shows several areas that women religious are most likely to say are "somewhat" or "very much" a challenge to them since entering their religious institute. These challenges are especially great for those who are the sole members of their ethnicity in the community where they live. Some 47 percent of these respondents, for example, say that not having their fellow members understand their culture is at least "somewhat" of a challenge to them. More than one in five list other aspects of their living situation that are at least "somewhat" of a challenge: that they do not feel understood by other members (28%), that their food is not welcome in the community (28%), that the members they live with do not accept their culture (23%), that they are asked too much to accommodate their culture to fit in the dominant ethnic/racial cohort (23%), and that they feel isolated or lonely (21%).

	All (N=618) %	Community with at least one other member of their ethnicity (N=474) %	Community where respondent only member of their ethnicity (N=55) %
Members who I live with not understanding my culture	18	14	47
Not feeling understood by other members of my institute	18	17	28
Feeling isolated or lonely	17	16	21
Members who I live with not accepting my culture	10	8	23
During my initial formation, my formator requiring me to accommodate my culture to that of my institute	9	8	17
My food not being welcome in my community	8	6	28
Feeling that I am asked too much to accommodate my culture to fit in the dominant ethnic/racial cohort of my institute	8	6	23
Not feeling welcomed by other members of my institute	8	7	12

Table 2.7. Respondent personally experiences the situation "somewhat" or "very much." *Source*: Data from Do, Wiggins, and Gaunt (2021).

The difference in reporting challenges is more obvious among religious members of the nondominant culture/ethnicity than among White members. While the majority of the White respondents report no challenges, the respondents of the nondominant culture/ethnicity report various challenges. One of the main challenges the respondents of the nondominant culture/ethnicity report is that their culture is not understood or accepted in their community. One significant factor is that their language and culture are not fully supported and accommodated. More critical is the racism in religious life that responding religious members encounter in their community.

Finally, the members of the nondominant cultural/ethnic background feel that they are expected always to adapt to the dominant culture in their community. Below are some of the comments written by those who do not live with anyone else of their ethnic/racial background.

> *My community did not challenge my classmates to accept things from my culture sometimes. For example, in initial formation you were to cook once in three months and so I would cook food from my country. Sometimes, the members of my community [would] all skip meals when it was my turn or another member from Africa's turn to cook.*

> *Because both of my parents come from cultures that are generally more "reserved" than "mainstream American" culture, I tend to communicate in a more restrained/less emotionally expressive way than most of the other sisters in our community. I think this has sometimes been misinterpreted as a lack of interest or enthusiasm. There have been some times when other sisters have made inaccurate assumptions about my views or feelings about various things based on my cultural background.*

> *Very different type of food from what I used to eat daily. Eating my preference is discouraged from the beginning to avoid special treatment.*

*An ignorance which can lead US-born sisters to say/do offensive
things. Some young sisters constantly ask you to say certain things
so they can hear it in your accent, then laugh about how it sounds.
Laughing at word choice from non-American English. All this is
almost always out of ignorance, not malice. Difficulty with being
understood and a perceived lack of patience from US-born sisters.*

*A deliberate resistance to learn about the problem of racism and
how to avoid it. One thing is to say that someone is ignorant.
Another to realize that that person does not want to know and
is actively working to remain ignorant. This is the most painful
thing I encounter: the desire to remain ignorant of the sufferings
of racial minorities in the United States and of solutions to solve
the problem.*

*It is not the outright racism that is a problem. It's the subtle
things that make you feel you always have to adapt to the dominant culture. This leaves me feeling isolated and uncomfortable
in my community.*

Summary and Conclusion

In summary, just as the cultural/ethnic diversity of the US
Church has grown more diverse, so has the diversity of the sisters residing and ministering in the United States. Nevertheless,
women religious are still more likely to identify as White (75%)
than the US Catholic population as a whole (52%). While newer
members of religious institutes are more culturally and ethnically
diverse than older members, women's religious institutes are still
in the beginning stages of learning to address cultural and ethnic
diversity in religious life.

Nearly eight in ten (78%) new members of women's religious
institutes say that their families had at least "some" impact on their
vocational discernment, with those who belong to the younger immigrant generations of sisters most likely to say their families had
"a great" impact. Most of the religious practices of their families

that impacted their discernment concern regular Catholic family life, such as participating in parish life as a family, prayer as a family, and their getting to know local priests, brothers, and sisters.

More than eight in ten (82%) new members of women's religious institutes say that a parish they attended had at least "some" impact on their vocational discernment. Among the parishes they identified as having the largest impact, one in ten was in another country (12%), with 71 percent of Black sisters identifying a foreign parish as having the largest impact. Their participation in the parish's Masses and liturgies had the greatest impact on their discernment, with those identifying a foreign parish most likely to say that being a liturgical minister, encouragement from the parish overall, and Masses and liturgies celebrated in their native language had a large impact on their discernment.

Those women religious who are the only members of their cultural/ethnic group in their local community or in their institute differ from others in how open they feel their religious institute is to accommodating diversity and how challenging they find life in their institute.

But the fact that more and more sisters from a wide variety of ethnic and cultural backgrounds are entering religious institutes in the United States today can serve as a witness to the larger society of how to create unity in difference while living together in community.

The next chapter explores another emerging trend in US religious life: international institutes of women religious who are establishing missions in the United States. Some come here to escape persecution in their home country or to minister to their own ethnic immigrant communities, as did many sisters of the nineteenth and early twentieth centuries. Others arrive with a desire to evangelize American culture, which they see as worldly, materialistic, and lacking in spirituality.

3

Patricia Wittberg and Thu T. Do

International Religious Institutes in the United States

Historical Background

As was noted in the introduction to this book, the first institutes of women religious to minister in the United States came from European countries. By the early twentieth century, some 420 institutes of non-contemplative sisters were ministering in the United States, but fewer than a quarter of them had been actually founded here. Most were either provinces of international institutes with motherhouses in Europe, or else had begun as houses or provinces of European institutes but later became independent.

Both "push" and "pull" factors contributed to the migration of religious institutes from Europe to the United States in these early years. Many were escaping persecution in their home countries. After the suppression of religious institutes in France during and after the French Revolution, unfavorable policies targeting the Church and its religious institutes spread throughout Europe. Many other European governments enacted similarly restrictive laws: Spain in 1820, Portugal in 1834, Italy in 1860, and the newly united Germany under Bismarck in 1873.[1] Sisters in these countries were often forbidden to accept new members or to engage in ministries, such as teaching schools. Such oppressive regulations pushed them to focus their energies on their overseas branches. In addition, many European religious institutes had more young women entering their ranks than they could employ locally: in nineteenth-century France, for example, four hundred new institutes were founded and already-existing ones were growing at a rate of 5.5 percent a year. Some 200,000 women entered these institutes between 1800 and 1880; 160,000 remained in France, but 84,000 went to their institution's houses or provinces overseas.[2]

In addition to these "push" factors, other institutes were responding to "pull" factors. French and German missionary societies published romanticized depictions of uncatechized Native Americans longing to be taught the faith or dire warnings that impoverished Catholic immigrants to the United States were in danger of abandoning the True Faith as a result of Protestant proselytization. These publications inspired young sisters to desire serving in American missions and superiors to send them there.[3]

Another "pull" factor encouraging European institutes to establish houses in the United States was the repeated invitations from bishops and priests to do so. Of the hundreds of European religious institutes that established houses in the United States during the nineteenth century, all but three had been invited by a bishop, a priest, or the superior of a male religious order.[4] These

1. Jo Ann Kay McNamara, *Sisters in Arms: Catholic Nuns through Two Millennia* (Cambridge, MA: Harvard University Press, 1996), 570; Joseph G. Mannard, "Maternity . . . of the Spirit: Nuns and Domesticity in Antebellum America," *U.S. Catholic Historian* 5, nos. 3–4 (1986): 312.

2. Patricia Wittberg, *The Rise and Fall of Catholic Religious Orders: A Social Movement Perspective* (Albany: SUNY Press, 1994), 84.

3. Wittberg, *Rise and Fall*, 103; Elizabeth Rapley, *The Lord as Their Portion: The Story of the Religious Orders and How They Shaped Our World* (Grand Rapids: Eerdmans, 2011), 294–95.

4. Wittberg, *Rise and Fall*, 84.

clerics were responsible for the spiritual and material welfare of the bourgeoning numbers of Catholic immigrants, and they established parishes, parish schools, and other institutions to serve them. Communities of sisters were needed to staff these enterprises once they were built, so bishops and other clerics made numerous visits to European motherhouses to persuade superiors to send sisters to the new country. Often lay Catholics, especially those in immigrant/ethnic parishes, pressured the bishop to invite sisters from their home country or invited them themselves.

Once the sisters arrived in this country, their institutes had many adjustments to make, both to the larger US culture and also to the differences in how Catholicism and religious life were lived here. Economic necessity as well as the needs of the people they served forced the sisters to modify or discard many of the cloister practices they had had to follow in Europe. The strong belief of Americans in equality was incompatible with the class distinction between choir nuns and lay sisters that had existed in many European institutes, and this practice too was eventually discarded by the institutes' branches after they arrived in the United States.[5] In a less-laudable adaptation, several institutes in pre–Civil War America adopted the American practice of owning slaves, to the scandal of their European superiors.[6]

Once the Americanized children and grandchildren of the original immigrants began to enter the institute, further adaptations took place. Community prayers and constitutions were translated into English, and some of the Old World customs and devotions that the younger generation found embarrassing or onerous were discarded.[7] Ministries changed too, since the descendants of the immigrants no longer needed separate schools, hospitals, or social service agencies to minister to them in the language of their

---

5. Patricia Byrne, "Sisters of St. Joseph: The Americanization of a French Tradition," *U.S. Catholic Historian* 5, nos. 3–4 (1986): 260.

6. McNamara, *Sisters in Arms*, 579–80.

7. Wittberg, *Rise and Fall*, 168.

ancestors. Many institutes were receiving far more entrants in their United States' province than in the mother country, and often these entrants were not of the same ethnic background as the original sisters of the institute. Difficulties of distance and communication, and pressures from bishops who wanted "their own sisters," eventually led many US branches to separate from their European motherhouses and become independent institutes. For many of the European-descended institutes at the end of the nineteenth century, one historian notes, the original French or German character of the institute "would have been hearsay" only.[8]

Contemporary Trends

Many, but not all, of these same dynamics affect the religious institutes that have come to the United States to establish a presence in the latter half of the twentieth century. Some continue to experience government limitations, or even persecution, in their home countries: several Vietnamese institutes, for example, moved to the United States following the unification of Vietnam under a Communist regime in the 1970s. Other institutes have come in order to serve co-ethnic immigrants to the United States: Korean institutes to serve Korean immigrants, Polish institutes to serve ethnic Poles, Mexican institutes to minister to the immigrants from their own and other Spanish-speaking countries, and so on. Some countries in Asia, Latin America, and Africa have experienced a growth in the number of women entering religious institutes, while the number of sisters in North America and Europe has decreased. The number of women religious in Honduras, El Salvador, and Guatemala has more than doubled between 1980 and 2016, while the number of sisters in Bolivia, Nicaragua, Paraguay, and Peru has also significantly increased.[9]

8. Byrne, "Sisters of St. Joseph," 260.

9. Julia Greenwood and Mary Gautier, *Trends in the Life and Ministry of Religious Sisters in Latin America: A CARA Special Report* (Washington, DC: Center for Applied Research in the Apostolate, 2018).

In Africa, the number of religious institutes has almost tripled, as has the number of women religious at the same period; religious institutes for women have also increased in number and size in Vietnam, Korea, India, and the Philippines in the last forty years (*Statistical Yearbook of the Church*). As a result, bishops in North America and Europe have often invited sisters from these countries to staff parish and diocesan ministries that the religious institutes in their dioceses can no longer sustain. For example, "Sisters from Africa and Asia who presently minister in the United States conduct religious education programs, work in Catholic hospitals and nursing homes, and serve in parish ministry."[10] One African writer puts the trend in this way, "In Nigeria, barely a century ago, Western missionaries, mostly religious sisters, educated Nigerian children; today Nigerian sisters reciprocate this same noble art of educating the young."[11]

Ideological reasons for establishing a mission in the United States are another "pull" factor that is similar to the motivation for religious institutes in the nineteenth century to send their sisters here. Today, the "developed" Western nations are often depicted to other parts of the Catholic world as suffering from a lack of spirituality and community in the face of rising secularism and individualism. In a sort of "reversed missionary action," sisters in Africa, Asia, and Latin America may see themselves as evangelizing countries that have lost religious knowledge and commitment, bringing the Gospel message back to the countries that had brought it to them.[12]

There are differences as well, however. The early nineteenth-century United States was a newly developing country that both wanted and benefitted from the service of the European sisters, who were often more educated than the local population. Laypeople,

10. Mary Johnson et al., *Migration for Mission: International Catholic Sisters in the United States* (New York: Oxford University Press, 2019), 175–76.

11. Caroline N. Mbonu, "Reversed Missionary Action: Prospects and Challenges for African Women Religious," *Religious Life Review* (July/August 2016): 224.

12. Mbonu, "Reversed Missionary Action," 221.

even non-Catholic laypersons, might pressure their bishop to invite them. This is seldom the case today. International sisters coming to this country, while often highly educated, may find that their professional credentials are not recognized here. As a result, they are often relegated to work as teachers' or nurses' aides instead of holding the professional positions they had enjoyed in their homelands. The United States is also less welcoming to immigrants in general than it has been in previous centuries, and many institutes experience difficulties in obtaining visas for their sisters to come here. The gap in wealth between the United States and the institutes' home countries means that some institutes send members here in order to earn funds for their ministries back home. Few, if any, of these factors were present when European institutes sent sisters here a century and more ago.

Nevertheless, numerous institutes in Asia, Africa, and Latin America have sent sisters to serve in this country. Some have erected only a single house here; others have established entire provinces. This chapter discusses the international religious institutes, originally founded outside of the United States, that have established houses, regions, or provinces in this country since 1965. These foundations may or may not currently belong to their original religious institutes in their home countries in terms of governance.

CARA has conducted several studies that help chart the presence of these newly arrived international religious institutes and their members. One study, in 2018, surveyed the international sisters living or studying in this country.[13] In 2020, CARA published another study of the international religious institutes from which these sisters have come.[14] For this latter study, which was

13. Thu T. Do and Mary L. Gautier, *International Religious Sisters Studying in the United States*, A CARA report (Washington, DC: Center for Applied Research in the Apostolate, 2018).

14. Thu T. Do and Thomas P. Gaunt, *International Religious Institutes Present in the United States since 1965*, A CARA report (Washington, DC: Center for Applied Research in the Apostolate, 2020).

commissioned by the Conrad N. Hilton Foundation in 2019, CARA gathered information about the institutes' characteristics and their sisters' experiences of arriving and ministering in the United States. Of 384 international religious institutes identified by CARA as having sent sisters to serve in the United States since 1965, a completed survey was received from 215, for a 56 percent response rate (see the appendix for details of the study). This chapter reports the findings from this study and, where possible, makes comparisons to another CARA national survey of religious institutes in the United States.

Canonical Status and Lifestyle

Like the other religious institutes that had arrived in the United States in earlier centuries, these recently arrived international institutes are categorized as being of either diocesan or pontifical right. While pontifical institutes are accountable to the Vatican, a diocesan institute owes its accountability to the bishop of the diocese where its motherhouse or leadership offices are located. Table 3.1 displays the canonical status of the international religious institutes of women in the 2019 study, compared with all the religious institutes of men and women emerging since Vatican II in the United States that were surveyed in 2017.[15] The international religious institutes are more likely than the US emerging religious institutes to be diocesan and thus subject to the authority of the bishop in their home country. As in the past, the provinces or regions of religious institutes in the United States may eventually choose to become a separate institute, but, among the international institutes in the 2019 study, half report that they still belong to their motherhouse in their home country.

---

15. Center for Applied Research in the Apostolate, *Emerging US Communities of Consecrated Life since Vatican II*, 3rd ed. (Washington, DC: Center for Applied Research in the Apostolate, 2017), 7.

	International Religious Institutes of Women (%)	Emerging US Communities since Vatican II (Both Men and Women) (%)
Pontifical	51	70
Diocesan	49	30

Table 3.1. Canonical status of international religious institutes. *Source*: Thu T. Do and Thomas P. Gaunt, *International Religious Institutes Present in the United States since 1965* (Washington, DC: Center for Applied Research in the Apostolate, 2020).

In addition to the distinctions between pontifical and diocesan canonical status, there are also differences categorized by the lifestyle of the institutes. In general, religious institutes have been characterized as "apostolic" (focused on a particular ministry or ministries), "contemplative" (focused on prayer), or "evangelical" (focused on evangelizing and spreading the Gospel). Nearly nine in ten international religious institutes are apostolic, followed by contemplative and evangelical. The survey asked institutes to select all categories that apply to them. Thus, the percentages in table 3.2 add up to more than 100 percent, because many groups placed themselves in more than one category. The majority of the international religious institutes were invited here in order to participate in an active apostolate.

	%
Apostolic	87
Contemplative	15
Evangelical	12
Monastic	2
Other	7

Percentages add up to more than 100 percent because communities/provinces may claim more than one community lifestyle.

Table 3.2. Lifestyle category of international religious institutes. *Source*: Data from Do and Gaunt (2020).

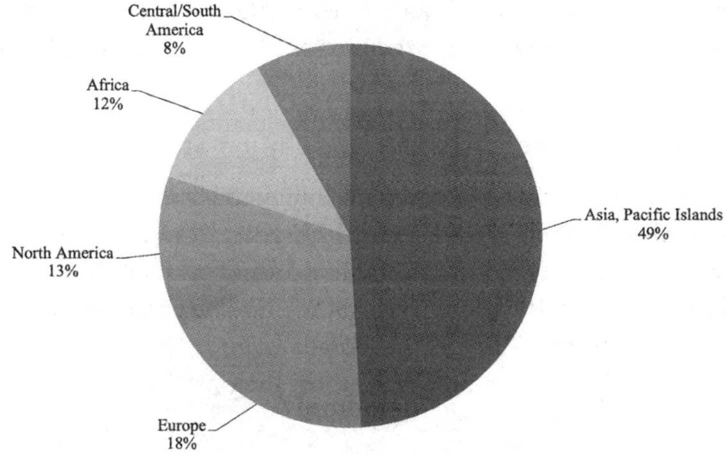

Figure 3.1. Regions of the world where international religious institutes were founded. *Source*: Data from Do and Gaunt (2020).

Continent of Origin

The international religious institutes that were founded elsewhere and have arrived in the United States since 1965 represent at least thirty-two countries. Unlike the institutes in previous centuries that mainly came to the United States from Europe, the largest sending continent currently is Asia (see figure 3.1). Almost half (49%) of the institutes in the 2019 study have come to the United States from Asia. Among these Asian institutes, the largest percentages come from Vietnam (51%), India (23%), and the Philippines (9%). Europe is the second largest sending continent, accounting for 18 percent of the institutes in the study. Among the European countries that have sent sisters here since 1965, France accounts for 28 percent, Italy for 24 percent, Spain for 21 percent, and Poland for 14 percent. International institutes from North America outside the United States come mainly from Mexico (95%). Africa provides 12 percent of the international religious institutes: Nigeria accounts for 37 percent of them, Kenya for 21 percent, and Ghana for 16 percent. Of the 8 percent of institutes that come from Central/South America, the three largest sending countries are Peru (21%), Argentina (15%), and Ecuador (14%).

Year of Arrival in the United States

The majority of the international religious institutes have come to minister in the United States within the past twenty-five years (see figure 3.2). Almost four in ten institutes came to the United States between 1965 and 1990 (38%). Six in ten arrived in the United States in 1991 or later (62%).

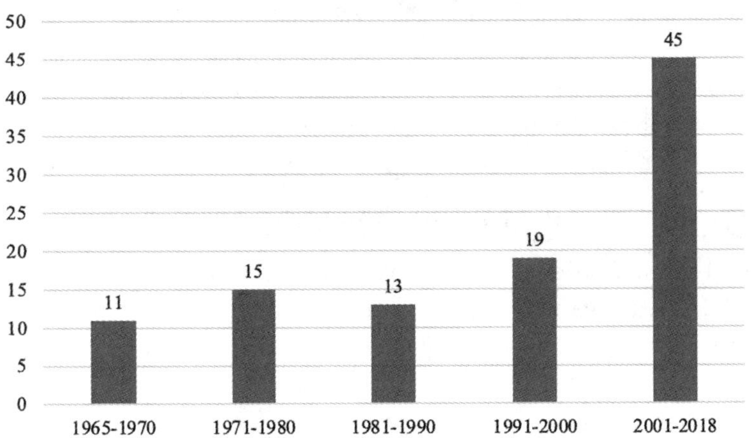

Figure 3.2. Year of arrival in the United States, by number of religious institutes. *Source*: Data from Do and Gaunt (2020).

We divided the year of arrival into two periods to compare the social environments in which the institutes arrived. The first period (1965–1991) was marked by rapid change in the Catholic Church and religious life as Vatican II was implemented, by economic growth and immigration from the Global South, by assimilation of American Catholics in society, and by a rapid decline in US entrants to priesthood and religious life, which resulted in the perceived scarcity of an available ministerial workforce for the

Church. The later period (1992 and later) has been marked by increased economic globalization, by increased immigration, and by a rising demand for religious from other countries to minister to both immigrant and nonimmigrant Catholics in the United States.

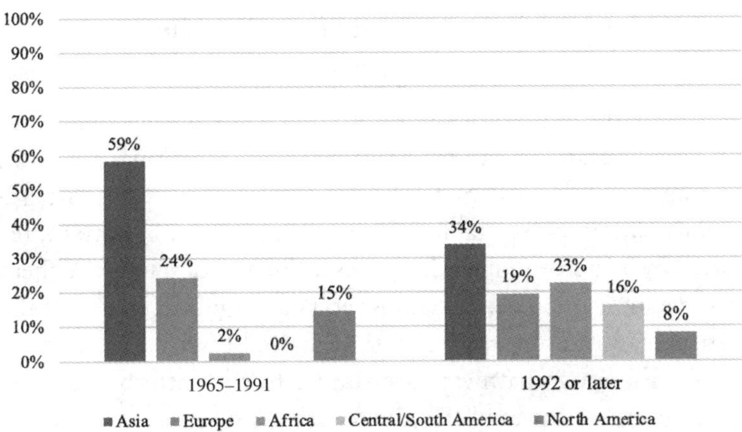

Figure 3.3. Region of origin of international institutes, by arrival period. *Source*: Data from Do and Gaunt (2020).

Figure 3.3 shows that in the decades immediately after the Second Vatican Council, the majority of international religious institutes arrived in the United States from Asia (59%), followed by Europe (24%) and Mexico (15%). Among institutes that came from Asia during this first period, about four in ten came from Vietnam (38%), followed by India (29%). The European institutes arriving in the United States prior to 1991 came mainly from Poland (40%), Italy (20%), and France (20%). All of the institutes coming from other parts of North America during this period were from Mexico.

These proportions shifted somewhat after 1991. The percentage of institutes from Asia coming to the United States fell from three-fifths to one-third, but still remained the largest proportion of those arriving. The percentage of North American (primarily

Mexican) institutes arriving after 1991 fell by almost half, while the percentage of institutes from Europe fell slightly. In contrast, the percentage of institutes coming from Africa and Central/South America after 1991 increased substantially.

Pathways of International Religious Institutes to the United States

As was the case with the international institutes coming to the United States in earlier centuries, the international institutes coming to the United States more recently have come through various pathways (see table 3.3). The most common pattern, reported by 37 percent of the institutes, is for a bishop to invite them to serve in his diocese. An almost equally large percentage of the institutes (33%) report that a priest invited them to serve in his parish. These two pathways are similar to the patterns followed by religious institutes in the nineteenth century.

	Overall %	Diocesan %	Pontifical %
A bishop invited us to his diocese	37	27	49
A priest invited us to his parish	33	34	31
We contacted a US bishop	16	18	11
Other	15	21	9

Table 3.3. International religious institutes' pathways to arrive in the United States. *Source*: Data from Do and Gaunt (2020).

One in six (16%) of today's international institutes, however, reports that it first contacted a US bishop, offering to minister in his archdiocese/diocese. One in seven (15%) came to the United States through another pathway (e.g., being invited by another religious institute). The pontifical institutes are more likely than the diocesan ones to report arriving in the United States because a bishop invited them. In contrast, diocesan institutes are more likely to report either that a priest invited them to his parish or that they had contacted a US bishop.

Members and Their Country of Origin

Conducting the project *Migration for Mission* in 2015, the authors identified over 4,000 international sisters who were born abroad but entered religious life in the United States.[16] Many of these, however, were members of US institutes. The 2020 study of international religious institutes located 1,700 of their members in the US (see table 3.4). Note that at least half of religious institutes identified for this study did not respond to the survey, thus the actual number of women religious in the international religious institutes who have a presence in the US is likely somewhat higher.

Candidates/postulants	80
Novices	51
Temporary vows/commitment	174
Final/perpetual vows/commitment	1,395
Total members	1,700

Table 3.4. Number of members. *Source*: Data from Do and Gaunt (2020).

On average, the responding international institutes reported seven members in initial formation (postulants, novices, and temporary vows) and eighteen perpetually professed members in the United States in 2019. Some of the nonresponding institutes may have no candidates/postulants, novices, or temporary professed members in the United States and so may not have answered the question.

The members of the responding international religious institutes are from thirty-four countries, representing five different

16. Johnson et al., *Migration for Mission*, 45.

world regions. As would be expected, the nationality proportions of the members belonging to these international institutes reflect the proportions of the institutes that have come from these countries. The majority of sisters are from Asia (43%). Among the Asian sisters, the largest number comes primarily from Vietnam (33%), India (28%), and the Philippines (19%). Africa makes up 19 percent of the members in international religious institutes, with Nigeria accounting for 26 percent, Kenya for 26 percent, Ghana for 21 percent, and Tanzania for 16 percent of the African sisters. In the international institutes from Central/South America, the largest percentages of members are from Peru (28%), Ecuador (17%), Colombia (17%), and Brazil (11%).

The international institutes from North America (i.e., from Canada or Mexico), however, show a different pattern. Two-thirds of their sisters are from the United States (67%), while far smaller proportions are from Mexico (23%) and Canada (10%). This may indicate that these institutes may be attracting women whose parents or grandparents came from Canada or Mexico but who themselves were born here.

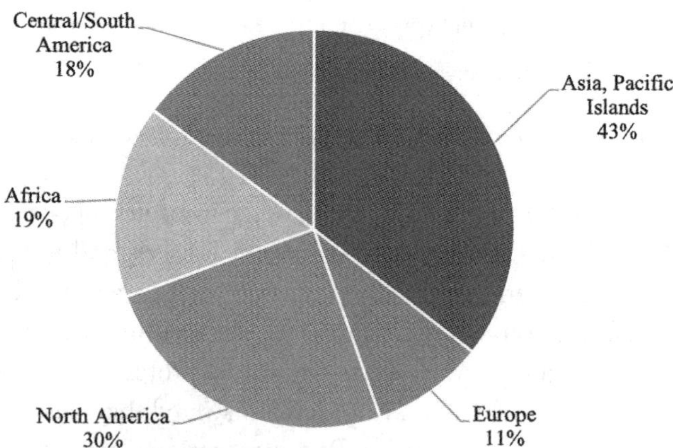

Figure 3.4. World regions of origin of the majority of the US community members. *Source*: Data from Do and Gaunt (2020).

Education

The members of these international religious institutes are highly educated, compared to the US adult population.[17] Six in ten members of these institutes have at least a college degree (60%), with four in ten earning a bachelor's or equivalent degree and more than two in ten a master's degree or higher (22%). A third have completed only a high school diploma or its equivalent. Seven percent report that their members have not even completed secondary school (see figure 3.5).

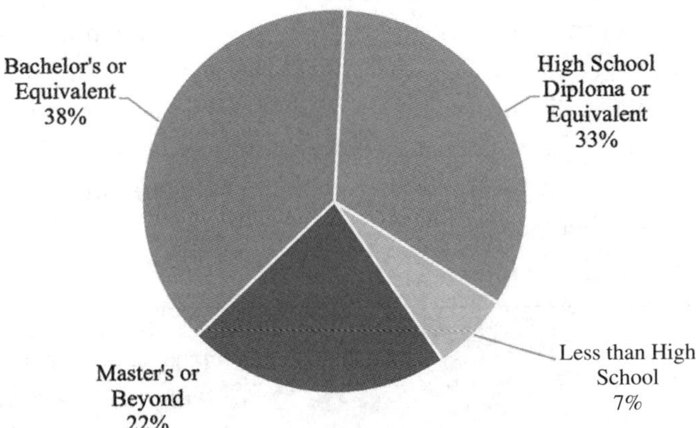

Figure 3.5. Highest level of education among members. *Source*: Data from Do and Gaunt (2020).

Many international women religious in the United States, therefore, are highly educated, but a substantial minority are not, while the overall population of the United States has become more educated. Accordingly, it is not always the case today—as it had

17. See American Community Survey, 2019, https://www.census.gov/programs -surveys/acs. Among the US population twenty-five years of age or older, 39% have only high school or less, 29% have some college, 20% have a bachelor's degree, and 12% have a graduate degree.

been in the nineteenth century—that the international sisters are better educated than those they served. Particularly for the four in ten international sisters with a high school diploma or less, this may cause problems. But even for the sisters who are highly educated, US accrediting agencies may not accept their credentials if they were earned at a non-US institution.

Legal Status

Women religious belonging to the international institutes arriving in the United States since 1965 hold various legal status. Similar to the previous study,[18] half of members reported by the institutes (48%) are US citizens. Three in ten (31%) hold legal permanent resident status. One in six (16%) holds a nonimmigrant religious worker visa. Just 5 percent hold another kind of nonimmigrant visa status, including student (F1 visa), tourist (B1/B2 visa), or other (see table 3.5).

	International Religious Institutes of Women (%)	International Religious Sisters (2019) (%)
US citizen	48	53
Legal permanent resident (green card)	31	25
Nonimmigrant religious worker (R1 visa)	16	13
Nonimmigrant student (F1 visa) or tourist (B1/B2 visa) or other	5	9

Table 3.5. Reported legal status of members belonging to the international institutes. *Source*: Data from Do and Gaunt (2020).

18. Johnson et al., *Migration for Mission*, 58.

Primary Ministry

Just as women religious in the United States performed a variety of ministries in the past, the sisters in international religious institutes also do so today. As shown in table 3.6, a third of the responding institutes indicate that their primary ministry in the United States is parish ministry. Nearly a quarter of institutes report their primary ministry is in health care (23%) and in teaching or educational administration (23%). Two in ten (18%) indicate that their primary ministry is social service. Twelve percent of institutes report ministering to their own ethnic/cultural group. Seven percent are contemplatives living in a monastery. Six percent indicate that their primary ministry is a diocesan office (e.g., vicar for religious, chancellor). Ten percent report serving in other ministries, most of which are spiritual direction or retreat ministries.

	%
Parish ministry (e.g., religious education, youth ministry)	34
Hospital/healthcare ministry	23
Education (teaching and administration)	23
Social service ministry	18
Ministry to our ethnic/cultural group	12
Contemplative ministry	7
Diocesan ministry (e.g., vicar for religious, chancellor)	6
Others	10

Table 3.6. Primary ministries of international religious institutes in the US. *Source*: Data from Do and Gaunt (2020).

Accepting US Vocations

The international religious institutes coming to the United States since 1965 have attempted to recruit new vocations and develop formation programs here. The majority of the international religious institutes (84%) indicate that they would accept vocations in the United States, and half actively recruit vocations here. Four in five religious institutes accept US-born candidates from other ethnic or cultural backgrounds than that of the country where the institute's motherhouse is located. About half of international religious institutes have a formal formation or initiation process in the United States before full membership (see table 3.7).

	%
Does your US community/province accept vocations in the United States?	84
Does your US community/province accept US-born candidates who do not belong to your ethnic or cultural background?	79
Does your US community/province actively recruit vocations in the United States?	53
Does your US community/province have a formal formation or initiation process in the United States before full membership?	45

Table 3.7. Vocation ministry of international institutes. *Source*: Data from Do and Gaunt (2020).

As we will see below, while not all international institutes have been successful in attracting vocations in this country, some obviously have, since three times as many of the members of North American institutes now come from the United States rather than from Mexico or Canada (see figure 3.4). This is not as true for institutes arriving here from other parts of the world.

Greatest Concern for Mission in the United States

When asked their greatest concern for mission in the United States, the majority of the international religious institutes report various challenges, such as carrying out ministries in this contemporary time, difficulty in expanding ministries due to the lack of support from the parishes/dioceses, difficulty in gaining legal status, and difficulty in recruiting new vocations in a culture that is different from their own.

Most of the international religious institutes that do not come from Canada or Mexico find it difficult to attract new vocations in the United States. Accordingly, these religious institutes continue to seek vocations from their original countries, as indicated by the survey respondents below.

> *Lack of candidates in the formation program is a major concern for us today. We also have to do much more in promoting vocations to priesthood and religious life for our communities.*

> *Our greatest concern is that it's very hard to get vocations from a local candidate, although we have tried many times to do the vocation promotion. Maybe because our target wasn't wide enough. So far, we only reach a few dioceses in California.*

> *Our greatest concern is how to get local vocations to join us in our delegation here in the United States.*

> *There is a lack of vocations in our community. I believe it is very difficult for all young women to join the life of consecrated life.*

> *Translating Schoenstatt and its charism into the American Church and society. This means finding young people willing to commit to this mission and work.*

> *With a slow number of vocations coming in from the United States, we have been recruiting vocations from Vietnam as well. We wish to continue our mission and respond to the many needs here in the United States with more vocations, but the numbers are slow to come in.*

Again, this is a very different situation from that faced by international institutes who sent sisters to the United States in the nineteenth and early twentieth centuries: at that time, the number of new American entrants rapidly surpassed the number of sisters from the old country. This is not now the case. One cause may be the increasing secularization of American culture. The religious institutes mentioned their concern for their mission of evangelization, how to keep the faith alive due to the changes in the socio-cultural context.

> *There is a lot of distraction and social pressure due to material wealth, and woundedness that requires qualified help and support.*

> *It is difficult to pinpoint one single concern, because the situation is quite complex; nonetheless, perhaps we could say the stranglehold that the secular culture places upon the family. In other words, the many different attacks that are being placed upon the family would be the greatest concern for our mission.*

> *Our greatest concern here is to keep the Christians' Catholic faith alive. And to be effective in our ministry to the Church and the people.*

> *Our greatest concern, as in all of our locations, is for the souls we work with and minister to. We are concerned for their holiness. We want to bring the light of Christ to everyone we meet. That can be very challenging living in a world that is far from Christ and offers many other distractions and temporary kinds of happiness. With these distractions many are unwilling to see the greatest gift we have in Christ and his Church.*

> *To carry out grassroots evangelization to the Church in America where it is possible, and where there is need for renewal of faith among the people of God in all kinds of situations or conditions, in line with the goals of the dioceses or archdioceses as the case may be, which is in line with the vocation we have chosen.*

The international religious institutes wish to expand their ministries; however, they report having difficulty doing so while receiving less support from the pastors and bishops.

We want to cooperate actively with the bishops and their dioceses, but at times it is not easy to be accepted for anything outside of strictly parish-based ministry.

Our community wishes to have enough facilities to welcome many retreat guests. At the same time, we wish to have more opportunities to open more convents and expand our ministries. But, it is sad to hear from the pastors that the Church cannot support the sisters because they do not have financial strength. We still hope and pray for every chance to extend God's kingdom.

It's also hard to find a suitable place like a bigger convent in a quiet place or a retreat center. Indeed, we need this kind of place in order for us to perform our ministry in a maximum way since our focus is on the spiritual formation (conducting retreats, healing ministry, prayer service, spiritual guidance, etc.).

The international religious institutes also mention concerns about navigating the United States' immigration laws on attaining legal status for members ministering in the United States. They describe the long waiting times and complicated paperwork. This, again, is different from the situation in the nineteenth century, when there were few legal restrictions or visas needed for those wishing to immigrate and work in the United States.

Our greatest concern is to get visas for the new members to come from other countries and to get a green card status.

Our greatest concern is the US Immigration law and changes. It's getting tougher and creates challenges in bringing more sisters for the mission in the United States.

Though there is need for us to serve, it takes a length of time for papers to be processed to catch up with the manpower needed.

Visa problems. Beginning struggles in establishing community here in the United States.

The international religious institutes are also concerned about the differences between the local culture and that of where they are from, including the language. In this, the new international institutes are similar to international institutes from previous centuries, whose members also had difficulty adapting to American culture.

> *To help the patients and make them comfortable through our work, listening to them and helping them to understand their situation of sickness. We also try to understand their culture in order to be able to help them and for them to understand us too.*

> *The creation of conflict among the sisters in terms of the liberal cultural differences as opposed to the African training and culture that is not so liberal, that causes authentic challenges for those missioned. Immigration issues also cause problems for new ones, which makes it difficult to transfer the older missionaries for more vibrant ones.*

> *If the priests who invited us are transferred, what will happen to us? As for those who will come after us, will they be able to survive in this foreign land?*

Another concern is the formation program for their members. The institutes cited the challenges of helping their members adapt to a new and different culture, how to help them to mature and grow emotionally, and how to prepare them to minister.

> *How to sustain the ongoing formation of sisters in order to be responsive to the current mission challenges; to witness to their consecration in more creative ways; to foster and promote vocations to consecrated life and to remain connected to the current development of religious life in Asia.*

> *Our greatest concerns in our North American territory include consolidation and fortification of our current members, vocational promotion, and ensuring financial sustainability for the future.*

> *Because our congregation is young and the members are also young, our main concern is that our young sisters who come here either for mission or for studies are able to withstand the challenges of the new culture and at the same time be able to learn from the rich, witnessing value of the older religious women here and not be distracted by the superficial attractions around them.*

> *Help young women enter in a theological life of faith, hope, and charity and accept to give up internal emotions.*

> *I would have the sisters complete their various courses as they continue to assist in pastoral work, mainly in the parishes.*

Summary and Conclusion

In many ways, the religious institutes that have come to the United States since 1965 come for similar reasons and face similar challenges as the religious institutes that first sent sisters to this country in the nineteenth century. Some are experiencing persecution in their home countries or have more young women joining them than they can support. As in the past, many are invited here by bishops and priests. They minister in many of the same ministries as sisters in previous centuries, and they experience similar difficulties in adapting to a new culture not their own.

But there are differences too. International religious institutes today are more likely to retain their diocesan status and accountability to the bishop of their home diocese. Unlike the religious institutes of the nineteenth and early twentieth centuries, which came mostly from Europe, today's international institutes come primarily from other parts of the world. Governmental and bureaucratic regulations hinder today's international sisters: visa restrictions that did not exist in the nineteenth century and credentialing standards that fail to recognize their educational training in their home countries. And while most of the international institutes that came to the United States in the nineteenth and early twentieth centuries rapidly attracted entrants from other ethnic backgrounds once they were in this country, this does not seem to be the case for international institutes arriving today from Asia, Africa, or Europe. In spite of these differences, international institutes are rendering valuable services that enrich the US Catholic Church today, just as sisters have done before them.

The next chapter features essays from two newer members in religious institutes in the United States today, whose voices echo and enflesh the themes from these first three chapters. One sister is a US member of a North American province of an international institute of women religious, with a presence in forty-one countries. The other is an African sister in a US-based religious institute.

4

*Juliet Mousseau and
Mumbi Kigutha*

Challenges of Newer Members in Communities of Women Religious

Survey data research is limited in its ability to capture the personal experience and voice of members of religious institutes. CARA invited two newer sisters to address the challenges of cultural diversity and generations in religious life as they have experienced it. They were asked to reflect on the challenges of the cultural and ethnic diversity of newer members, of diminishment and growth, and of evolving ministries and community structures.

Sister Juliet Mousseau, RSCJ

Entering religious life today is a challenge from the beginning. It is relatively rare for a young woman to choose religious life over the other options, in part because few Catholics today grow up knowing women religious. When one chooses to enter a religious order, the isolation of not being understood or supported by friends and family is the first obstacle to overcome. After that, the power of God's call takes over, and we find the supports that we need to live to joyful fulfilment. Yet, as everyone knows, choosing the right vocational path does not eliminate challenges.

Here I'd like to highlight three groups of challenges that newer religious embrace upon entry to the convent: those that center on the changing demographics of religious life, adaptation of communities to meet multigenerational and intercultural needs, and the internal and external shifts involved in deinstitutionalization. As I expand on these three areas, I wish to note that my perspective is limited by my realities: I am a White American of European ancestry, in my forties, professionally trained. While newer religious find many things in common, the challenges I face are certainly not the same challenges faced by older or younger entrants, women of color, or women with different levels of education than I have.

The first most obvious challenge I encountered on entering religious life was the rapidly changing demographics. I entered my community twelve years ago at age thirty and made final vows in 2020. My congregation, the Society of the Sacred Heart of Jesus, is an international community in forty-one countries, and my province is comprised of the sisters in the United States and Canada. Today, the average age of sisters in my congregation is seventy-eight to eighty. A congregational study revealed that within the next fifteen years, the numbers will drop dramatically, and we are already seeing the ramifications of rapidly aging sisters. We have had to adapt to the need for different types of communities and a real migration of sisters from active ministry to retirement homes. Houses that once served small groups of sisters are now inaccessible to those with mobility issues. Homes that once held eight sisters require more maintenance than the remaining three sisters can manage. The physical makeup of many of our community homes no longer meet our needs.

While I described this change above as a "dramatic drop in numbers," the reality that we face is one of loss and grief, in which my sisters and friends face the ultimate transition to be embraced by our loving God. As newer members, we are becoming experts in mourning and loss, in building relationships that we trust will span the gap between this life and the next.

On a more practical level, the demographic changes mean that we need to adapt in our multigenerational communities as needs and ministries change. Our close relationships with sisters as they experience the natural process of aging, including changing abilities and needs, places us in caregiving roles. Holding full-time ministry along with the weight of concern for our elders is unsustainable, and we must clarify roles and boundaries for ourselves. To continue living in multigenerational communities, we must use our imagination and creativity. We need to have the freedom to ask for professional assistance when grocery shopping or heavy cleaning become too demanding on an aging community. We need to foster deep relationships of trust and shared identity among religious of different generations. We are striving for multigenerational communities in which the younger sisters are supported in the mission and the sisters who have retired find meaning and purpose in their volunteer and prayer ministries. This meeting of needs is a point of real tension among us.

Our households are becoming more diverse in other ways. Newer religious mirror the cultural and ethnic diversity of the younger members of the Catholic Church in the United States. While older generations, especially the "bubble" who are in their seventies and up, reflect the diversity of Catholics in the first half of the twentieth century (largely of Irish and German ancestry), more recent immigration trends have changed the shape of today's incoming classes of religious. Newer religious grew up in a more diverse society, and we expect to find it within our houses. Yet, the increased diversity has also brought cultural challenges and a demand for cultural competency. Over the last decades, initial formation has included cultural education. Cultural diversity is a gift to us, not only for the visible beauty that it provides in food, artistic expression, and music, but also for the deeper values that it brings to our attention. My experiences living with sisters from Latin America, Africa, and Asia have shown me the value of doing things together rather than always acting on my own. The American values of individualism and independence need to be countered with the togetherness that a communal culture can illustrate for us. Intercultural households stretch our concepts of what is "normal" and allow us to open to new ways of doing things, which in turn brings us more freedom.

Cultural diversity is an important gift, and at the same time it challenges us. A diverse community easily highlights blind spots in our welcome and acceptance of others. How open am I to letting my routine be changed in order to meet the needs of a sister whose expectations are radically different from my own? Beyond helping a newcomer navigate a new situation, am I willing and able to eat, pray, and recreate differently so that she feels more at home in a foreign culture? It is easier for me to see the small adaptations I make than it is for me to recognize the giant changes she has had to make. Cultural diversity in community life might mean that I (and all those in the dominant culture) have to become less comfortable in my home so that someone else feels welcome there.

In addition to the multiculturality of the Church in the United States, religious men and women around the world continue to create community together. Especially during this year of pandemic, organizations such as the International Union of Superiors General (UISG) in Rome and the Catholic Theological Union in Chicago have brought together women and men in online forums to discuss topics of interest. The experience I have in the Society of the Sacred Heart, both living with sisters from other countries in the United States and living abroad with our sisters, has helped open my heart to the diversity of the world and the needs of people far and near. When the tsunami struck Japan in 2009, a sister from Japan was visiting us, and we shared with her the grief it caused her. Ministering in southern Spain among migrants from Africa, I learned firsthand the plight of populations on the move around the world today. When a sister from the Philippines recently died of Covid-19, we mourned with the sisters in her country because she was our sister too, and many of us knew her from the time she spent in our country. The needs and joys of the world become ours when we have a personal connection to them.

Finally, younger religious are facing the question and challenge of deinstitutionalizing religious life. Newer religious experience a different relationship with ministry than previous generations. In the last half of the nineteenth and first half of the twentieth centuries, women religious entered communities that were experiencing a boom of membership, which allowed them to build and maintain magnificent institutions of education and health care. Without the untiring work of women religious in the United States for over a century, this country would have lacked basic education for children and health care for all. They ran the charity organizations that helped people from all walks of life, especially the waves of migrants who arrived in North America with nothing. By the mid-twentieth century, women religious were well established and widely recognized for their commitment to the outcasts of society. The older generations who are still living entered religious life in the midst of this heyday. They experienced full novitiates and widespread recognition.

Religious life has shifted dramatically over recent decades. Many institutions have closed or been handed on to lay leadership, though often religious communities retain some control over the identity and charism of the ministry they once operated. Sisters who have long held positions of authority and leadership struggle to step back even when it is well past the arrival of a new stage in life. Newer members witness the incredible generosity of these sisters and their gift to the Church. At the same time, generous commitment can easily overflow into workaholism and a ministerial reality and commitment with the desire for strong and lasting community relationships. A shift in recent conversations about religious life is helpful here. The uniqueness of religious life is not found in the activity and ministry of religious men and women. The unique identity of religious life has to be found in *who we are* rather than *what we do*. We are women and men who have dedicated our lives to God, in service and love for our fellow human beings and all of God's creation. The love of God and hope for God's ultimate reign is what we bring. Our commitment to loving relationships and hopeful presence permeates our actions whatever we do, and those key elements of our life allow us to shift our focus as the world changes around us and demands our attention change.

Another challenge as religious deinstitutionalize is the absence of a corporate witness. Previous generations have experienced the energy and enthusiasm of working together to create something new for God. This generation is witnessing the withdrawal of sisters from ministries, and rarely do we work with other religious in a group of our own congregation. Institutional ministries are largely a thing of the past. Yet, newer religious find ways to work together in paid and volunteer ministries across congregations. A major example of this reality can be found in Giving Voice, a grassroots organization that gathers women religious under age fifty to support one another and form community. Out of this gathering of women religious of all different congregations and charisms, like-minded sisters have joined to write a book on religious life today, to go on retreat together, to form intercongregational communities, and to both witness and minister on the border with Mexico. The desire for intentional corporate ministry takes on new energy and vision in this generation.

Women and men who answer the call to religious life today are entering into a reality that is rapidly shifting, a microcosm of the rapidly changing world community. The decisions we make today will either prepare us for the world of the future or put us further behind. Smaller, multigenerational and intercultural communities, unconnected to large institutions like hospitals and schools, will help us to be flexible and reactive to the calls of God and the world.

Sister Mumbi Kigutha, CPPS

I first came to the United States in the late summer of 2006. Arriving at the Philadelphia airport that night, I was glad to find two of my "American" sisters waiting for me: one was originally from a Caribbean country but had been in the United States for a very long time, and the other was a Tanzanian sister who had arrived three weeks prior. I was tired after an almost eight-hour layover in Amsterdam, then flying into Tennessee before landing in Philadelphia. We loaded my luggage into the van's boot (which I would learn to call a trunk) and set off to what would be my home for the next three years. On the way, we stopped at a petrol (gas) station with a food court so I could get some take-away (takeout) for a late supper (dinner).

The teller (cashier), without a pause to breathe—or so it seemed—greeted me and asked what I'd like to order. The Caribbean American sister stood patiently at my side, reassuring me that I should get whatever I wanted. I was overwhelmed by the array of choices, some familiar and some not, by the speed at which the cashier spoke and her difficulty in understanding my accent. Tired and overwhelmed, I felt humiliated by the cashier's lack of patience, but I am ever grateful that the sister at my side acted as an ally, ensuring that the cashier communicated directly with me even if it did take a little bit of extra time.

Feeling misunderstood or misheard was an enduring challenge. I ran into more language problems when I registered for school, because my written English was judged to be "wrong," when in fact, I fell back to what I was familiar with, which is British grammar, British punctuation, and British sentence construction. The different names for everyday items, the liberal use of sarcasm—which I've still not gotten the hang of, and which often strikes me as rude—the variety of American accents, being told repeatedly that I can't be understood or that I am mispronouncing words, the expectation to speak systematically and in great detail in order to be understood, believed, or taken seriously. I have found that Americans rely heavily on verbal exchanges to communicate. I have also learned, however, that politeness is not always sincerity. I cannot tell you how many times I've been told, "*We have to have you over for dinner*" with no follow-up.

That first night in America, when I arrived at my new community, everyone was already in bed, and those who had picked me up also bade me goodnight as soon as they had given me a cursory tour of the space I would call home for the next three years. So I decided to take a shower before trying to sleep myself. In the bathroom, I stood in the stall for a while, trying to figure out the taps (faucet) to get the water to the right temperature. Then, as I stood under that stream of water, my tears finally fell. I was not just crying because I was tired from travel or because of the sum total of my experiences since arriving in the country, but all that had happened and what I had had to endure to get me to Reading, Pennsylvania, that balmy night. It was the endless visa application forms, the hefty application fee, arriving at the US embassy in Kenya at 5:00 a.m. to queue up with others on a similar mission, in the cold and exposed to the elements, all in order to make a 7:00 a.m. appointment, then sitting in the interview hall with mounting anxiety, hearing others summoned to counters and overhearing their conversations and subsequent disappointment or joy. It was finally hearing my number called and arriving at the counter, where a glass divider demands that you raise your voice to be heard. It was being asked what the first three books of the Bible are and where St. Peter is buried, to verify my status as a member of a religious congregation, and wondering in amazement whether the embassy official was serious in asking me such questions. It was bidding farewell to my family and all that is familiar and travelling abroad alone for the first time. It was a fellow passenger amazed that I spoke "good English" as an African, not realizing that such remarks would occur more frequently than one would imagine and would continue to be an enduring hallmark of my American life, but that in equal measure, my accent would also be used to discount my language skills. It was the fear approaching the unsmiling customs officer in Tennessee and answering yet another set of questions to be allowed entry in the country. Standing in the shower under that glorious warm water, with my mother's admonition of wasting water and electricity running through my mind, I wondered how I was going to survive the next three years.

Survive I did. I even managed to thrive in various ways; however, as I later learned, this hasn't been the case of many immigrants, including immigrant religious women and men. I attribute my somewhat success to the steady diet of books, movies, and sitcoms that had offered me varying glimpses of American life over the years, my mother and brother who had preceded me to this country at different times and had shared their experiences with me, but also that Caribbean American sister who became my formator and friend and who loved and guided me with infinite patience through numerous ups and downs. Three years later I professed and returned to Kenya. But my relationship with the United States was not over. Six years later, after discerning with a new congregation, I was on my way to Dayton, Ohio.

This time, I knew what to expect, to a certain extent, and how to prepare, not just for the immigration bits, but to make my adjustment easier. Carrying art, clothes, food, and various items that reminded me of home was a priority. I also chose my flights more wisely, choosing an airline that is consistently voted among the best in the world to make my trip more comfortable, allowing a short transit time for the first leg and slightly more time at my port of entry in order to navigate customs.

There was still a healthy amount of trepidation in me, as I would be the first African sister to ever join my congregation, and my encounters with prejudice and racism had already scarred me from my first stint in the United States. But I arrived to an amazing welcome from the sisters, some of whom had reached out prior to my arrival by e-mail, something that I appreciated very much. I arrived just as we were beginning our annual congregational gathering, which meant that the following few days I met a lot of sisters, eager to welcome me.

There have been challenges to being the pioneer African member and also one of two pioneer Black women in a predominantly White congregation with German roots and an American culture. The German roots emerge in many of my sisters' work ethic, where busyness and extremely full days seems to be the norm, where efficiency and effectiveness seem to be the hallmark of excellence, and where tasks are always completed way before the deadline. None of these things are necessarily bad, but they can be a challenge for someone coming from a culture that values spontaneity in scheduling, an open-door policy to friends and acquaintances, and investing more in relationships than productivity. Another challenge has been finding ways to honor my elders (I'm younger than most of my community members) in a country that so values individualism and independence. My attempts to help or assist have been rebuffed many times, even considered offensive. Hand in hand with that, however, is that my own thoughts, dreams, and ideas have not been given the weight that I would desire. I consider this to be one of the things that will most challenge the transition to the next era of American religious life, as the same ol' is chosen time and time again, instead of letting go and creating space for new and emerging ideas. American exceptionalism has influenced American congregations, and the voices, opinions, and ideas of newer and fewer members are drowned in the "our way" attitude, opinions, and decisions of the older American White majority. There has been an unspoken expectation for me to go along with decisions made concerning me despite that not being our usual way of proceeding, an expectation to assimilate, to fit in, to earn my place, which is counter to who we proclaim to be or what we proclaim to desire.

At times I was bombarded with a whole lot of questions, which felt intrusive. Everyone was curious about their newest member. In fairness, I was quite different from anyone else. Questions about my educational and economic background and personal details about my family members are not, however, what I would consider appropriate for a first conversation—especially at dining tables with four to five strangers looking on and listening. Friends visiting me from back home also encountered questions like "Do you have running water at home?" soon after a "Hi, and what's your name?"

Lack of orientation to community life and congregational culture, systems, and policies remains an enduring challenge. Before me, there hadn't been a new member for more than ten years and thus the majority of our members had a common orientation, having been involved themselves in deciding policy and structural changes. The gaps in transmitting that knowledge have been significant and are most apparent reactively after I have made mistakes. I am eternally grateful that I had spent time in the United States before and that I'm naturally curious and independent, because I have had to learn to find my way many times. The one thing I'll probably never get over is the amount of paperwork this country requires. Not just in the numerous doctor's visits I made in my first weeks but also what the congregation required of me as a new member, not to mention the continuous humongous amounts of immigration paperwork. It's quite overwhelming and hard to navigate through without guidance or explanation of its importance. Another challenge was going for the psychological evaluation and finding a practitioner who was still undergoing her own training. The fact that she clearly wasn't culturally sensitive and her constant struggle to understand my accent and the very obvious misrepresentation of me in her final report had me despairing. As I had gone through the process and after reading the report, I knew that she had been prejudiced, but at that time, more than four years ago, racism, bias, and prejudice were not mentioned with the increasing ease that has occurred due to ongoing and relentless activism by so many.

What continues to sadden me, however, is that my experiences and challenges have not in any way been used to alter the experience of those that have come behind me, making me wonder whether the verbalized desire for interculturality, for diversity and inclusivity, for antiracism is true or whether it has become the politically correct thing to utter. I am also constantly heartbroken when I am misquoted, my words or actions judged negatively when language and communication could lend much clarity and clear the air, so to speak. When language through gossip and rumors has been used to discredit me and chip away at my reputation, I always learn of such events after the damage has been done.

I had heard of Midwestern politeness, and I couldn't quite fathom what it meant until recently as I spent time in reflection and realized that I leave so many conversational spaces confused about whether the conclusion was a no, a maybe, or a yes. There is constant word crafting and wordsmithing in religious life from the experiences I have had so far in various circles. It creates constant turmoil for the recipient of the communication, however, because apart from creating confusion about outcomes, it can be used to deflect from arriving at the "why" of any decision made concerning them. The failure to communicate clearly and succinctly, to explain why or why not has also left me many times unable to anticipate, grieve, and/or celebrate. Language is power as it can uplift, build, affirm, and also sadden, destroy, and control. Looking ahead, my hope is that we shall start living into a future where language will be used to clarify and welcome, redistribute power, reconcile, protect, and free newer, minority members. Even though St. Francis is said to have stated, "Preach, and if you have to, use words," language is the gift that clears misunderstanding and bridges the hidden nuances of our diverse backgrounds.

Summary and Conclusion

In the voices of Sister Juliet and Sister Mumbi we hear clearly the challenges of community demographics, generational divisions, and deinstitutionalization. Sister Juliet reminds us that "the unique identity of religious life has to be found in *who we are* rather than in *what we do*." In all its various forms, religious life is a life of witness. Sister Mumbi prods us to acknowledge that it is easier for us to speak of interculturality than to confront and change our behaviors and words to act with interculturality.

This concludes the first section of this book, describing the new waves of women religious in the United States. Through research and personal stories, these chapters describe the changing demographics and other challenges that newer members in religious institutes confront. They also describe the continuing appeal of religious life and the similarities of these newer members to the generations that have come before them. The remainder of this book describes institutional changes in governance and collaboration among institutes as they continue to come to terms with new realities of religious life. As in the first section, the book presents both research and personal witness to describe and illustrate trends in religious institutes and religious life.

Changes in Governance and Collaboration

5

Michal Kramarek and
Patricia Wittberg

The Evolution of Leadership in Religious Life

The first section of this book chronicles the changing demographics of the new waves of religious sisters. Recent trends include the growing cultural and ethnic diversity of younger members that contrasts with the more homogeneous composition of the older generations. This diversity has become more pronounced in recent years because of the sharp decline in US-born vocations and the continued increase in non-US vocations. The primary reason for these developments is that a number of religious institutes founded in the United States have international missions or provinces whose non-US members now outnumber the US membership.

In consequence of those trends, religious institutes in the United States increasingly face new challenges related to governance and collaboration in ministry. One of those challenges is that institutes founded in the United States may need to reassess where the motherhouse should ultimately be located and what the implications are of the evolution of the institute's leadership from older, mostly White, US-born sisters to the younger, foreign-born, culturally and ethnically diverse sisters. Long-standing international institutes may have to consider whether different cultural expectations affect how leadership will be exercised by leaders drawn from other parts of the world.

In order to explore these challenges, we take a closer look in this chapter at the historical evolution of leadership in religious life. Next, we describe factors that are currently shaping the evolution of leadership, including the geographic spread of religious institutes beyond the United States as well as the international origin and training of new members. Having established this context for the ongoing transition of leadership, we identify and describe the most important characteristics for members of institutes' leadership teams and the main challenges institutes face while discerning new leaders. In the chapter's conclusion, we offer some practical recommendations and discuss the implications of the findings.

Historical Evolution of Leadership in Religious Life

Throughout their history in the United States, religious institutes of women have had to deal with challenges arising from cultural differences in their membership and leadership. During the nineteenth century, differences arose when the expectations of superiors in France, Germany, or Poland clashed with the American culture of the sisters entering the institute in this country. Americanizing adaptations such as relaxation of cloister, elimination of the inferior class of lay sisters, and praying in English rather than in French, German, or Polish often led to the American branch splitting from its European foundation and becoming a separate institute.

Even when the institutes adapted to American customs for their membership, however, changes in leadership were slower to occur. Not until the 1980s and 1990s did some US institutes begin to elect sisters to leadership who were not of the same ethnicity as the institute's founders had been a century earlier.[1] And inter-

1. Margaret Susan Thompson, "Sisterhood and Power: Class, Culture, and Ethnicity in the American Convent," *Colby Library Quarterly* 25, no. 3 (September 1989): 174.

national institutes with provinces in numerous countries around the world have only recently begun to elect leaders who are not from their European or North American branches, in spite of the fact that the majority of their entrants now come from Asia, Africa, or Latin America.

Expanding leadership and membership to fully include different cultures is, therefore, not an easy task. The next section of this chapter will explore how religious institutes are dealing with these challenges today.

Membership

The Geographic Spread of Religious Institutes

Unless stated differently, the findings presented here are based on the 2019 CARA study, *Forming a New Generation of Leadership for Religious Institutes*. This study included a national survey of the leaders of US-based religious institutes, a series of four focus groups of leaders of international religious institutes with provinces in various areas around the world, and three individual interviews with the leaders of the US regions of international institutes. (See the appendix for a more detailed description.)

Among major superiors of US-based women's religious institutes, three in five (62%) oversee communities that are solely living and ministering in the United States. The remaining two in five (38%) have geographical jurisdiction over an area both within and outside the United States, which means that they govern provinces or missions in other countries.

The canonical status and the number of an institute's internal units affect how the institute moves into different parts of the world and the forms of governance it creates once there. Three-quarters of US-based women's religious institutes (76%) are recognized as religious institutes of pontifical right, which means that they are subject to the Congregation for Institutes of Consecrated Life and Societies of Apostolic Life in Rome. As would be expected, religious institutes that have jurisdiction of provinces or regions both within and outside the United States are more likely than those present only in the United States to be organized as religious institutes of pontifical right.[2]

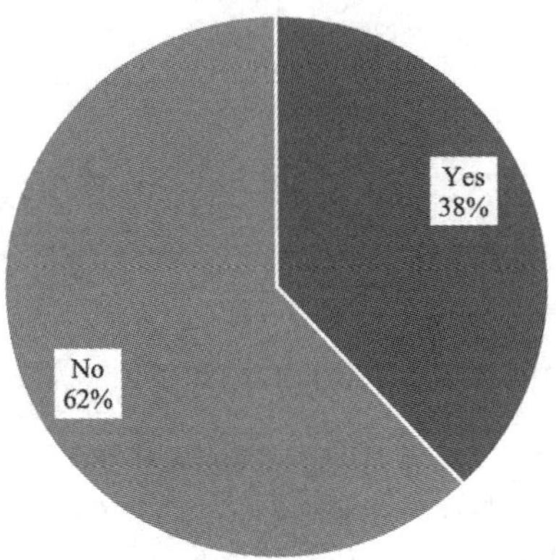

Figure 5.1. Does your unit's geographical jurisdiction cover area both within and outside the United States? *Source:* Patricia A. Wittberg et al., *Forming a New Generation of Leadership for Religious Institutes* (Washington, DC: Center for Applied Research in the Apostolate, 2019).

One in seven (14%) of the institutes surveyed is an institute of diocesan right, which means that it operates under the authority of the local bishop. Relatively few (4%) are public associations of the faithful that have not yet received full canonical recognition. Another 3 percent are monasteries that are separately governed (although they may participate in a federation), and 1 percent functions as societies of apostolic life organized around a particular work or apostolate whose members often do not make traditional perpetual religious vows.

2. Specifically, 86% of institutes with provinces or regions outside the United States are organized as institutes of pontifical right, as compared to 71% of institutes present only in the United States.

Of the 249 women's religious institutes that participated in the study, 15 percent have houses or provinces in South America, with a total number of 401 members living there (see table 5.1). One in ten has houses or provinces in the other North American countries of Canada and Mexico (11%), in Europe (10%), or in Central America (10%). It is less common for US-based women's religious institutes to have houses or provinces in Asia (8%), Africa (6%), or Oceania (4%). In terms of specific countries, US-based women's religious institutes are most likely to have houses or provinces in Mexico (fifteen institutes), Peru (thirteen), Brazil (twelve), and Canada (twelve).

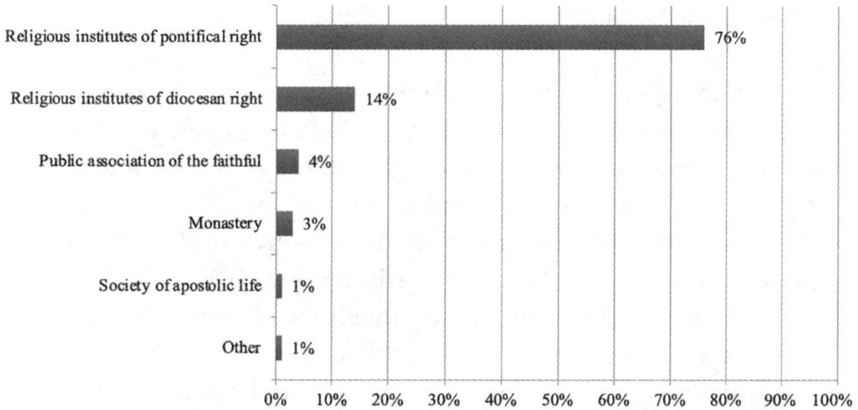

Figure 5.2. Canonical status of religious institutes. *Source:* Data from Wittberg et al. (2019).

While the largest percentage of US-based women's religious institutes participating in the study have houses or provinces in South America, the largest number of members (472) reside in Europe. The countries with most members include Brazil (298), Mexico (209), Poland (188), Canada (168), and the Philippines (157).

	Institutes		Total Members
	%	#	#
Europe	10	26	472
South America	15	37	401
North America	11	27	377
Asia	8	19	340
Africa	6	14	212
Oceania	4	11	191
Central America	10	25	135

Table 5.1. Top three countries in which the unit has jurisdiction. *Source: Wittberg et al. (2019).*

According to the focus group members and the interviews, a primary purpose in establishing a mission in a new country was often to attract vocations from that country. This was true of the European institutes that had established missions in North America during previous centuries, and it is true of the current European and North American institutes that have established missions in Asia, Africa, and Latin America more recently. Sometimes establishing such a mission resulted in numerous members entering the institute in that given country, and a new province was eventually established. Other times, however, it did not. As one religious sister noted:

> *The Peruvians, we have had quite a few enter but only the one has persevered. So, they came, they maybe made it to temporary vows, and then they left. The one sister who is Peruvian remains. . . . The idea was, when we started the mission, that if it flourished, it would be to serve that country. But the reality is she is just the one person.*

At other times, however, many new members entered an institute from the mission country. The institutes had various ways of adapting to this situation. The sisters' institute in an international family of priests', brothers', and sisters' institutes has a formalized procedure for establishing local, self-sustaining units in new countries:

> *We usually wait until we are sure that we are going to be permanently there, that there is a mission there that we can sustain. . . . Like in Mexico we said, "We will make a commitment then, for Americans to remain there until there are enough local vocations and those women are formed enough that they can be in vocation [ministry]." So, now we just have one American left in Mexico, we have one left in India, we have none left in Bangladesh; they are all indigenous sisters.*

An American congregation of sisters, in contrast, had to carefully negotiate a new governance structure, once their Asian sisters began to outnumber the American ones:

> *So we grew together over time and eventually recognized that we can't keep [saying] "the [American] congregation and [Asian country mission]," that we need to be the [Sisters of X]. And so that's when we made the second province in the United States and kept the Generalate. But the very last general chapter we had was in [Asian country], because every other chapter alternates. At that chapter one of the big questions was, "[Asian country] is growing; they are almost two hundred strong." Your median age then was in the late forties and the United States was getting smaller: our median age was in the seventies. We didn't have as many missions. They were opening missions and we were closing missions. They were having vow days and we were having funerals. And so how do we continue, and there was a big question about should we separate and become two congregations.*

The sisters decided to remain one congregation, and even made provision for the establishment of future provinces should the occasion arrive:

> *Our constitutions defined, when we restructured, that whichever province—and it does not say "[Asian country] and American" because someday there may be an Ecuadorian province. But whatever province the general superior is from, the first councilor must be from a different province.*

The respondents in both the survey and the focus groups, therefore, come from widely varying experiences in how their institutes incorporate members from other countries and mentor them to eventual leadership roles in the institutes.

The Origin of New Members

Nine in ten superiors of women's religious institutes (87%) accept new members to their unit (i.e., congregation, province, monastery). The remaining 13 percent said that they do not. The survey respondents were next asked whether their institute recruited candidates for membership from outside the United States. Such recruitment had been common as recently as the 1940s, when US-based institutes made frequent trips to Ireland and other European countries specifically to invite young women to travel to America and become religious sisters.

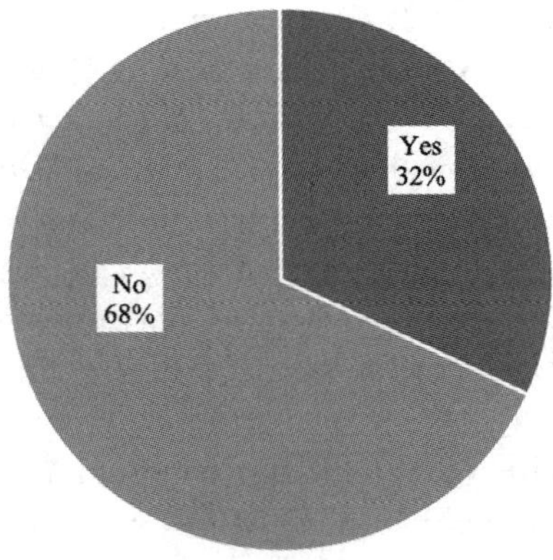

Figure 5.3. Does your unit seek out candidates outside the United States? *Source:* Wittberg et al. (2019).

Overseas recruitment is less common today but still occurs. As shown in figure 5.3, approximately one-third of the institutes seek out candidates outside the United States (32%). The remaining 68 percent do not search for vocations in this way. In contrast with earlier periods, however, it is primarily institutes with houses or provinces outside the United States that are more likely to say that they recruit candidates from other countries: 66 percent do so, as compared to only 12 percent of the institutes that are located solely in the United States. Among these latter institutes, the entrance of candidates from abroad is more *ad hoc*, as several of the sisters mentioned:

> *Then we have this young woman from South Korea who is going to become a novice. She got to know us through CTU. She did her doctoral studies, she got a D.Min. at CTU, and her advisor was Fr. [name]. . . . And as she was talking about her desire for religious life, he directed her to us.*

Recruitment from overseas, whether currently or in the past, affects the membership composition of an institute. Survey respondents were asked how many perpetually professed members are currently in their unit (their institute, province, or autonomous monastery). Those who answered this question report having, on average, 105 perpetually professed members in their unit. An average, however, can be distorted by one or two very large numbers at the top of a scale. A better measure is often the median, the number at the exact middle of a sequence. In the table below, while the average (mean) number of perpetually professed sisters is 105, the median is much smaller (sixty perpetually professed sisters). This indicates that half of the superiors report having fewer than sixty members in their institutes, and the other half report having more. In actuality, the number of perpetually professed sisters reported for the various institutes ranges from two to 939 sisters (see table 5.2).

	Mean $\#$	Median $\#$
Total number of perpetually professed members	**105**	**60**
Of the above, total who entered religious life outside the United States	16	1
Of the above, total number who are age sixty-five or younger	5	0
Total number currently in initial formation	**3**	**1**
Of the above, total number who were born outside the United States	2	0
Of the above, total number who are age sixty-five or younger	2	0

Table 5.2. Number of members. *Source:* Wittberg et al. (2019).

The survey then asked how many of these perpetually professed sisters had entered the institute outside of the United States and how many were aged sixty-five or younger. Again, on average, the respondents report having sixteen sisters who had entered religious life outside of the United States, but this number is distorted by a few respondents who report non-US membership in the hundreds. A more accurate estimation is the median number, which shows that half of those who responded report having either zero or only one perpetually professed member who had entered religious life outside of the United States. Similarly, while the institutes report an average of five members aged sixty-five or younger, half of those who responded had no members who were that young.

When compared to religious institutes that are present only in the United States, units with geographical jurisdiction both within and outside the United States are larger and contain a greater number of younger members. The latter institutes contain, on average, eighty-five more perpetually professed sisters than the former, twenty-six more perpetually professed sisters who entered religious life outside the United States, and seven more perpetually professed sisters who entered religious life outside the United States and are age sixty-five or younger.

The major superiors of women's religious institutes were also asked to report the total number of prospective members who are currently participating in initial formation as postulants, novices, or temporarily professed members. As table 5.2 shows, the average number of new entrants is three, but, again, this number is distorted by a few large responses. Half of the respondents report having either none or only one member currently in initial formation.

Again, when compared to those units that are present only in the United States, responding institutes with geographical jurisdiction both within and outside the United States report, on average, five more sisters currently in initial formation, four more members currently in initial formation who were born outside the United States, and four more sisters currently in initial formation who were born outside the United States and are age sixty-five or younger.

As the focus group participants noted, however, simply reporting the total number of members who entered religious life outside the United States obscures some important differences. Several of the leaders of institutes located in this country reported having members who, although they were born in the United States themselves, had parents who had immigrated here. Others had come to this country as small children and considered themselves as belonging to both cultures:

> *Some of them are born in Vietnam: the second-year novice right now was born in Vietnam, came to the States at age fifteen, and basically has lived here the rest of her life, educated here. Our vocation minister was born in Vietnam, came here—I am not exactly sure how old she was when she arrived—studied here, but the women who are attracted to us now, we have a fair number of Vietnamese sisters that are attracted. And they may or may not come directly from Vietnam or just be first generation themselves.*

Training of New Members

Once a young woman has entered a religious institute, she participates in several years of spiritual formation and training. This period is commonly called "initial formation." The survey asked whether all of this training occurred in the United States or whether some or all of it occurred elsewhere.

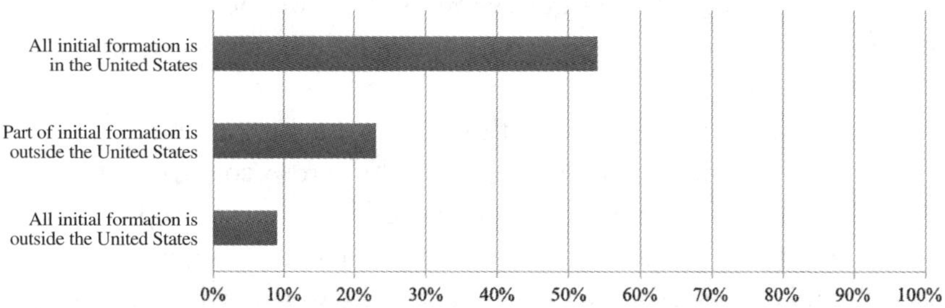

Figure 5.4. Does your unit offer initial formation outside the United States? *Source:* Wittberg et al. (2019).

Over half of women's religious institutes offer all initial formation in the United States (54%). As would be expected, units that are present only in the United States are more likely than units with geographical jurisdiction both within and outside the United States to offer all initial formation in this country.

A quarter of units offer part of initial formation outside the United States (23%), but units with geographical jurisdiction both within and outside the United States are more likely than those only present in the United States to do so.

Only one in ten offers all initial formation outside the United States (9%). And, again, units with geographical jurisdiction both within and outside the United States are more likely than those present only in the United States to do so (see figure 5.4).

The focus group participants and two interviews described some of the variations in the locations where their newer members received their initial formation. In one international institute,

> *Yesterday we had initial profession for sixteen women. Our international novitiate is here, so one from Mexico and the others are from Africa and Asia. . . . The candidate program, or the postulants, whatever you want to call them, that is all in their country. The discerners, the postulants, stay there. They come here for two years and then they are missioned back either to their original areas or, if they feel they have a missionary call, to wherever they are called.*

One US religious institute of sisters did not establish a mission overseas until the early 1960s, but its need for an overseas formation program surfaced almost immediately:

> *The [first] two [novices] came over here and at the end. Mother [name], who was Mother at that time, called them into her office and asked them what they thought about this and the one [novice], who is now our General Superior, said that she thought that the novitiate should be in [Asian country], and Mother [Name] listened to her. I think that is a real good story.*

Having new members from different countries than the present membership has led to cultural discrepancies in the past. The survey did not ask questions about such cultural differences within present-day institutes. The topic did arise, however, in the focus groups. Sometimes there were clashes within the formation programs in other countries:

> *So, we have in one province Bangladeshi and Indians who have very different cultures, and it doesn't always go smoothly. But they are learning from each other and what we are trying to talk about is "What is our [institute] culture that is an umbrella over whatever culture we are in?" Because all the countries we are in were very multicultural and so now we are working on becoming intercultural in terms of the way we live, and then also in terms of saying, you know, "it's not 'your culture better, my culture better'; what we are trying to live is a [institute] culture."*

The focus group participants were unanimous in saying that, because of these cultural differences, the initial formation of their new members had to be done either partially or completely in the members' home countries, or at least in the area, by formation directors who were themselves of the same culture. But, in general, they expected that the formation directors themselves would have had professional training, usually in the United States:

> *Most of our formators have been formed at CTU [Catholic Theological Union in Chicago], even though they are indigenous to other countries. We have had some who have gone to Kenya, but it's only recently that there are any opportunities for formation leadership in these other countries, for training people. South America, CLAR has excellent programs.*

When the majority of the new members entering a religious institute begin to come from a different culture, this will change how the institute's charism is interpreted. The focus group of sisters who had established their first province in an Asian country only within the past fifty years was optimistic that these changes were beneficial. As one of the Asian superiors in the focus group said:

> *So, you can add, I think, that [the] charism is [the] same thing. But the expression is, could be different in different countries because in this country we talk with these people who live here and our charism. So, it must concern this situation and the lifestyle and thinking style with this charism and this charism is for this people and this charism [is the] same charism but made for this people in a different situation and different historical idea so we learn with the charism how they think, how they live and adjust it.*

One of the participants in that same focus group, however, made a point of staying behind afterward to report that the Asians in the group were politely omitting some of the early conflicts.

She reported resistance among the American sisters when their Asian province was first raised to coequal status:

> *You know, "Will we have to take our shoes off when we enter chapel like [they] do? Will we have to learn to eat [their food]? Will we have to learn [their language]?" There was a lot of resistance to that, such that when this current structure of two provinces with an overarching Generalate was first established, there was a worry that, "Heaven forbid that the head of the community be [an Asian member]."*

Allowing a newly multicultural membership to reinterpret an institute's charism will inevitably result in tensions.

Leadership

Qualities of Leaders

The major superiors of the women's religious institutes were asked how important various leadership qualities were to them and how serious various hindrances or challenges were to discerning and calling forth new leadership. As shown in figure 5.5, virtually all responding superiors believe that prudential judgment and time management skills are important for the leaders of their institute to have (99% and 97%, respectively). Nine in ten of them (94%) believe that fluency in the English language and conflict management/resolution are important. And four in five major superiors (84%) believe that human resource management skills are important.

Half of the major superiors (46%) believe that fluency in other language(s) is at least "somewhat" important for members of their institute leadership team. And one in ten (11%) believes that this was "very" important. Superiors who have jurisdiction both within and outside the United States were more likely than those present only in the United States to consider fluency in a foreign language to be "very" important.

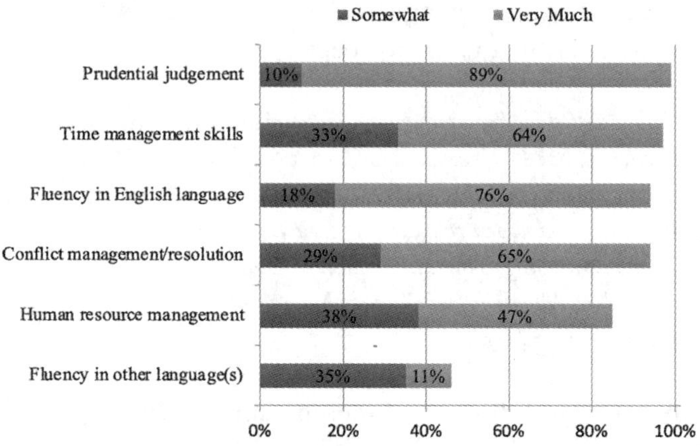

Figure 5.5. How important are these characteristics for members of your institute leadership team? *Source:* Wittberg et al. (2019).

While the expectation of fluency in other languages is relatively low now, knowledge of Spanish, Korean, or Igbo, for example, may rise in importance if the majority of the members begin to come from an institute's formerly peripheral provinces or missions.

Challenges or Hindrances

In terms of challenges or hindrances in discerning and calling members to leadership, the major superiors of women's religious institutes were most likely to be "somewhat" or "very" concerned about the lack of leadership training/experience among potential new leaders (74% of the major superiors), reluctance among potential leaders to assume new leadership (74%), and the lack of leadership skills among potential new leaders (70%). (See figure 5.6.)

Several of the focus group respondents agreed with the survey respondents about the importance of these challenges. One of the leader's institutes had set up a mentoring program:

> *We have a liaison from the general leadership that mentors or is a link between the provincial and the Generalate. So, they have no power, but they are just a communication kind of person and*

also for us a mentoring kind of person because the leadership in these other countries is younger and they don't have as much experience. So, if they have a question, "How do you do this?" they can call somebody here who is not the superior general and get some advice and answers.

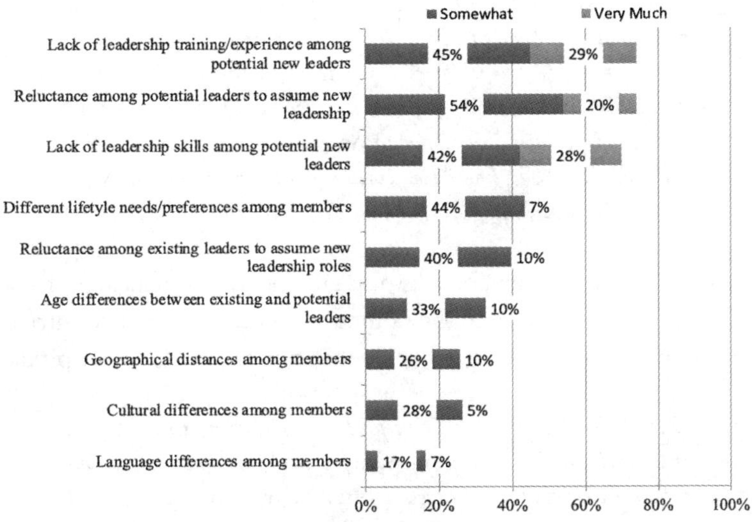

Figure 5.6. How much are these a challenge or hindrance to your institute in discerning new institute leaders? *Source:* Wittberg et al. (2019).

One of the leaders, interviewed separately, mentioned deliberately calling forth the strengths of the newer members:

Part of that is how we go about forming committees, that we make sure that we invite, nudge, encourage the new people to serve on committees, different people. And challenge them if they don't step forward, to challenge them.

The focus group participants also agreed that there was a reluctance among their non-US members to assume leadership roles in the institute. For the leader of the sisters in a family of priests', brothers', and sisters' religious institutes, this reluctance was tied to the demands of leadership in the institute's local ministries:

> *It's a feeling that if they are old enough and have the experience, they need them more in the countries where they are. So, anybody who could have those kinds of [institute leadership] positions is in a major position in their country so they are either the provincial or they are the head of schools that are the major institutions in those countries and it's very difficult to get them to keep their names in. . . . It's like, if they are pulled out of there that could put that institution in jeopardy. So, it is very hard. And again, we talk about that, like, "The world is more important than your area." However, [laughter] that is very hard for people to do.*

A leader in another focus group cited a strong distaste among younger members, both in the United States and in other countries, at the prospect of managing their institute's schools or hospitals:

> *One of the things that was helpful to me in going through [the international leadership program] was the number of women who were from other cultures. All over really, Colombia, Guam. I was in a group with a sister from Guam. I have learned so much from those sisters in terms of how differently they see their congregations and how differently they see leadership and how differently they understand religious life going forward. It has no big corporate footprint at all connected to it. And that is something that they see is almost repellent to their desire to be in leadership.*

Another leader suggested a way of dealing with this reluctance:

> *So, it's a matter, then, of learning from one another, and seeing how it develops in some people that are in leadership as well as how it [is] developing within the individual person. As far as anything specific on leadership, I think we do it more subtly, so we don't scare people off and not have anybody want to come.*

As figure 5.6 shows, the superiors also listed other challenges besides lack of leadership skills or reluctance to assume leadership. Those challenges include different lifestyle needs/preferences among members (considered a challenge by 51% of major superiors), reluctance among existing leaders to assume new leadership roles (50%), age differences between existing and potential leaders (43%), and geographical distances among members (36%).

Only a third of major superiors (34%) believe that cultural differences among members are at least "somewhat" of a challenge or hindrance to their institute in discerning new institute leaders. The major superiors of women's religious institutes who have jurisdiction both within and outside the United States are more likely than those present only in the United States to consider it to be "very much" a challenge.

Several focus group participants also cited cultural differences among the members as a challenge. Some thought that these could be overcome by becoming more aware and respectful of these differences:

> *I think that it's more to remember that leadership for cultures is much more than language and food and dress and all of that. It's ways of thinking and ways of being. If the Church is going to grow, they have to understand that the Church is not going to remain Roman either; it's going to be different and religious life is going through this and it could be a gift to the Church to be able to say, "This is possible."*

Finally, the last challenge captured in the survey was the language differences among members, a concern for a quarter of major superiors (24%). Additionally, a challenge that was not listed in the survey at all was raised by several respondents in the focus groups and interviews. This challenge involved the increasing difficulty of obtaining a visa to visit or live in the United States. This applied both to the difficulty that general superiors from another country might have carrying out their supervisory duties in the United States as well as the difficulty entire institutes might have in establishing a common US formation year for their new members from other countries:

> *The plan was for them to come here to the States, here in [city],*
> *and we have a house in mind and we were going to create that*
> *as a formation house. So, it would be very international. . . .*
> *Our stretch is that we have been having great difficulty getting*
> *visas. I guess this is the name of the game, and unfortunately even*
> *this morning that is what I was working on. We have submit-*
> *ted one of the applications and it was returned saying that they*
> *needed a site visit. And since then we have heard from, last week,*
> *Homeland Security telling us that we needed—believe it or not,*
> *but I will show you the notebook; it is about three inches thick*
> *that we submitted—that they need some further information*
> *in three different areas and so I have been working to get this*
> *done and resubmit it.*

Implications and Recommendations

The survey did not ask any questions regarding the implications of forming a new generation of leadership in religious institutes from members in a wider range of countries. The focus group members, however, were well aware of them:

> *I would say that people understand that the future is not in the*
> *United States. Again, we have tried to look at the history and*
> *say that perhaps the reason that we are diminishing is so that*
> *the world can grow in other places. Where, if we kept being the*
> *dominant culture, that might not happen as easily. It's still hard*
> *because people wish there were vocations from the United States*
> *but there are not.*

> *As I think about this too, we are going to be so much smaller in*
> *the future, the leadership styles that are beginning to emerge will*
> *be more effective than that corporate mind-set that we've got,*
> *the large group mind-set.*

As a result, the interviewees and focus group participants had several practical suggestions, drawn from their own experience, for other institutes who anticipate having leaders and members from other cultures:

Inclusion: Several focus groups recommended formalizing structures of inclusion for both governance and members. *"Like the steering committee, that is half and half. On [planning] the 150th anniversary, it's half and half. So, I think we have made deliberate decisions together." "So, we passed legislation that said that whatever the percentage of North Americans that are going to come to the chapter, the same percentage of [Africans] have to come."*

Transparency: *"To the degree that you can be transparent about what you are doing, why you are doing it, how you are doing it, that's how others learn. And that doesn't mean that they have to imitate, but they begin to understand that there was a process involved which led to this."*

Get to Know Each Other's Culture: *"I think the thing that breaks down the walls most quickly is to get to know them. Because if there are just times for them to get together, then that begins to break down [walls] because then they begin to see them not as 'them' but as people, 'They are my friends.'" "The four American sisters, when they came to our country, they tried to learn [our] food, culture and respect us. That means that they rooted this charism in our field, acculturation."*

Mentor for Cross-Cultural Awareness: *"I would hope that there would be a relationship where you mentor the person because—think of all the different forms of legalities that we have in this country that anybody coming from [another country] would have no clue about."*

Mentor for the Practical Aspects of Leadership: *"[X] is a good program, but one of the things they have to incorporate better in that program is a much clearer sense of the practical nature of leadership. There is not much training in that program, which has a thing to do with how you cope with that. Or how you become creative with it."*

Summary and Conclusion

The Catholic Church is currently undergoing a profound demographic change: the number of adherents in North America and Europe is shrinking while numbers are increasing in the Global South. Religious institutes, increasingly, are reflecting these changes. In many ways, this cultural shift in religious institutes' membership and leadership resembles a similar shift in the nineteenth and early twentieth centuries, when Irish, French, German, Polish, or Italian institutes established missions in the United States. Eventually, their new American members reinterpreted the original European charism and ethos of the institute to fit American culture. In time, even the leadership of the institute shifted to the American membership, or the US institute separated from its European parent. Will the same thing happen today, as the majority of an institute's membership increasingly hails from India, Kenya, or Brazil? Or will the institutes develop and witness to a new appreciation of its multicultural identity? To quote the leaders in the focus groups:

> *I think the sisters here are very excited about the fact that the international novitiate is here because it gives them the balance, saying "We might be diminishing here but we are growing in other places." It's more that the importance is [the charism]; the importance is not in this place.*

> *Because of the multicultural backgrounds of us, they expand our charism. So, we become richer.*

Witnessing to the richness of intercultural living may be a new and much-needed ministry for the future of today's fractured world. The next chapter describes another powerful witness that religious institutes are providing to the world today—that of restructuring their governance in light of the changes in religious life.

*Jonathon L. Wiggins and
Thomas P. Gaunt*

Restructuring Governance in Religious Life

Over the centuries, the number of women responding to a vocation in consecrated life has ebbed and flowed depending on social, economic, political, and ecclesial circumstances. The past fifty years have seen dramatic changes in the number, ages, and geography of women religious in the United States and throughout the world. While the governance structures of women religious institutes might not seem like the most applicable topic to describe the changes occurring in the institutes, they do in fact reflect the strains those institutes are experiencing.

A CARA study for CommunityWorks, Inc., of institutes of women religious in the United States who are redesigning their governance structures, for example, found that many institutes are making changes due to the diminishing number of sisters they have in the United States.[1] A sister in one of those institutes encapsulated the challenges, saying:

1. Thu T. Do, Jonathon L. Wiggins, and Thomas P. Gaunt, *Governance Structure: Survey of Members of the Leadership Conference of Women Religious*, A CARA report (Washington, DC: Center for Applied Research in the Apostolate, 2020). See appendix for details of the study.

> *We are aging and diminishing in numbers in [Canadian provinces] and our US provinces. Our structure was designed for a larger, younger [institute]. It needs to be reimagined to meet the needs of our younger cohorts.*

While a diminishing number of sisters in the United States is the most common problem, it is manifesting itself in institutes in different ways. The two most frequent scenarios are illustrated in the two brief vignettes below. The first features an institute that has seen an increasingly steep decline in members over the past five decades and struggles to remain focused on its charism and ministry when so many of its members, resources, and facilities are now devoted to the healthcare needs of its remaining, mostly elderly sisters.

> *Established in the United States in 1938, this religious institute reached its peak in membership in the late 1960s (202 sisters) and has been steadily declining in number ever since. Now with the sisters having an average age of eighty-one, only two new members have entered in the past two decades. Twice in past decades, a number of leadership positions were eliminated as the ratio of those in leadership to those in ministry approached two to one. Also worrisome has been how to maintain the few facilities they have not already sold, how to take care of the health needs of the remaining twelve members, and how to plan well for the institute's eventual closure.*

The second vignette gives an example of different trends in US religious life, involving the issues of geographic dispersion, leadership not being proportionately representative of the cultural and ethnic diversity of the members, older members dominating leadership positions, resources not being where they are needed for ministries, and centralized leadership that does not adequately understand or respond well to the needs of those in ministry on another continent.

Established in 1920 in the United States, this institute reacted to a rapid decrease in members during the 1970s and 1980s by establishing missions in two African countries. With membership in those countries increasing in the past four decades, two provinces were formed, one in the United States and one for the three African countries. The [institute] headquarters, however, remains in the United States and leadership positions are currently disproportionately held by older, White US sisters. African sisters complain that institute leaders do not understand or respond adequately to the needs of the sisters actively engaged in ministry. US sisters, on the other hand, find the healthcare needs of their older members dominating their attention and resources.

While these two examples certainly do not describe all institutes in the United States, they do cover a great number of those institutes who are or have been restructuring their governance.

In this chapter we broadly examine how the changes in membership number, age composition, and geographic dispersion have been challenging religious institutes' governance structures and how the institutes have responded.

Declining Numbers, Aging, and Geographic Dispersion of US Membership

Decline in the Number of Sisters

The number of sisters in the United States reached a peak in 1965 with 181,421 sisters (*The Official Catholic Directory*, 1966). That number has been steadily declining since then, with 41,357 sisters reported in 2019. This sharp decline is seen in practically all of the religious institutes in the country. And, while much alarm has been voiced about the number of priests (both diocesan and religious) declining by 40 percent from 1970 to 2019 (seen in figure 6.1), the number of religious sisters has declined almost twice as steeply—74 percent—during that same time period.

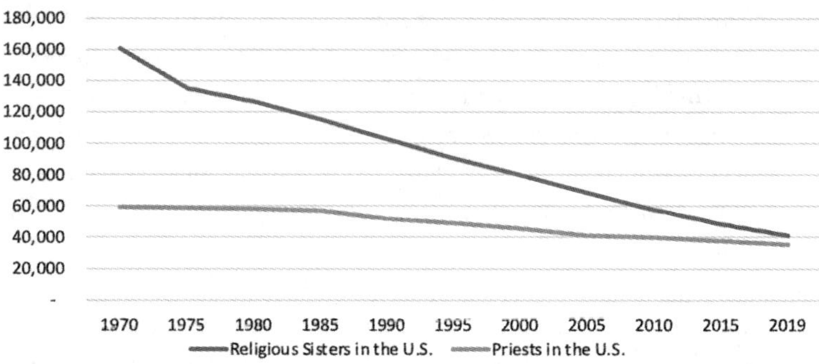

Figure 6.1. Number of religious sisters and priests in the United States, 1970–2019. *Source:* Data from CARA, "Frequently Requested Church Statistics," http://cara.georgetown.edu/frequently-requested-church-statistics/.

This rapid reduction in the number of sisters in the United States has greatly impacted the leadership of these institutes. Among institutes that are completely or mostly US based (as in the first vignette above), leaders are grappling with how to manage their institutes' reductions in sisters available for active ministries and likely eventual closures. A sister from one such institute in the CARA/CommunityWorks, Inc., study wrote: "No new members in over twenty-five years."

For those also experiencing member growth in another country or part of the world (as in the second vignette), it has meant needing to redistribute power and resources from the United States to the places that are experiencing growth and that still have a relatively large number of sisters in active ministry. For both types of scenarios, however, it has meant the need to change how their governance is structured in the United States. As one sister explained: "[Our] structures are meant for a group of 12,000 and now we are 3,000."

Age Distribution

A stable and sustainable age distribution for the members of a religious institute would be expected to have the largest number of members at the youngest end, gradually declining decade by decade (primarily due to departures and deaths) until reaching the oldest end, when the number of members would decline quickly in the last decades of life. Such distributions were common up to the 1950s in the United States. During the 1960s, 1970s, and 1980s, though, a large number of members left religious life while the number of new members entering decreased sharply. By the turn of the century, the age distribution of sisters had reversed itself, with a large and growing number of members among the oldest and a small number among the youngest.

Table 6.1, which projects the number of US religious sisters from 2015 through 2035, was developed by CARA researchers in 2016. One can see that the majority of sisters (55%) will be eighty or older by 2025, with only 15 percent under age seventy. By 2035, about seven in ten will be eighty and older. Already, however, the pool of sisters who are readily able to engage in full-time active ministry and serve in leadership roles is small, and it will continue decreasing in number in the following decades. As one sister in the CommunityWorks, Inc., study stated as a reason for redesigning her institute's governance structure: "Need to be proactive in structuring ourselves for a dramatically different demographic reality in fifteen years."

	2015	2025	2035
Under age 40	1%	<1%	<1%
Age 40 to 49	2	3	<1
Age 50 to 59	6	4	7
Age 60 to 69	22	9	7
Age 70 to 79	32	30	14
Age 80 to 89	26	37	40
Age 90 and older	11	18	31

Table 6.1. Current and expected age distributions of religious sisters in the United States. *Source:* Data from CARA's US Sisters Projection (unpublished, 2016).

The previously existing structures of governance for religious institutes assumed that the majority of members are able to engage in full-time active ministry and leadership. When a majority of members are limited in their participation in the institute's life and mission due to age or infirmity, the previously existing structures need to adjust to that new reality.

While this reality is greatly affecting all religious institutes of women, the type of impact it has varies. Those institutes that are primarily US based, for example, find themselves having not enough sisters of an age to be active or semi-active in ministries and/or leadership roles. As one sister stated, the challenge they are really facing is the "[d]emographics of the sisters in the United States (e.g., aging of sisters, fewer sisters qualified as leaders)."

US institutes that have experienced growth in numbers on other continents have a different challenge as they face the same issues for their aging sisters in the United States, while having many sisters who are active or semi-active in ministry in other countries. For them, having the institute headquarters, most of the leaders, and many resources located in the United States while the majority of ministries are occurring in another place becomes problematic. As one sister summarized their challenges: "The aging of members in North America and the youth of members in Africa and South America requires a new perspective on governance into the future."

Geographic Dispersion

In the latter half of the twentieth century, religious institutes generously responded to the needs of the Church across the United States and across the world by missioning groups of sisters to establish communities and works in locations far from their motherhouses and traditional regions of ministry. While some of these new communities and works attracted local vocations to the institute, many did not. As the years have passed, institutes have been faced with various challenging situations, such as a few elderly sisters living and ministering as an individual community on another continent, or the reverse situation of having most of the younger sisters living and ministering in a different country from the older sisters and motherhouse (as in the second vignette).

Data from the CARA/CommunityWorks, Inc., study of six institutes of women religious in 2019 and 2020 that were undergoing or had just completed restructuring their governance illustrates such a change. When asked for the major countries where their sisters currently serve, the six institutes listed more than fifty countries, many of which are Asian (such as India and the Philippines), African (such as Uganda and South Africa), Latin American (such as Brazil and Peru), or European (such as Italy and Germany).

The two institutes of the six with the highest percentages of members ages seventy or older have a majority (80–89%) of their members in the United States. The three with the lowest percentages of sisters ages seventy or older (50–60%) have at least two-thirds of their members in countries other than the United States. As would be expected, the resulting new governance structures of these two different kinds of institutes will be radically different. A sister from an institute experiencing growth on another continent described their situation in this way:

> *Given our charism of being missionaries in the African world, more of the younger members of the [institute] are in Africa. In Europe and America, there are mainly sisters who retired from the mission in Africa. Aging in Europe and America challenged the leadership in matters of the age of the sisters who were carrying responsibilities in leadership and finances. It was becoming difficult for them to carry out effectively the service of leadership.*

Yet another sister summed up how a reconfiguration of their governance structure needed to happen to help resolve some of these issues, including financial ones:

> *Inequality in the number of nuns in the Provinces of the Regions and their ages. Examples: (1) Numerous provinces with economic possibilities, with good leaders but with a majority of*

> *old religious and (2) smaller provinces with younger religious,*
> *with few financial resources and lack of leadership experience. It*
> *was not easy to exchange religious between the Provinces—even*
> *with temporary collaborations—if not everything went through*
> *the General Government.*

With the declining number of sisters, the aging of the sisters in the United States, and the dispersion of members that some institutes are experiencing as a backdrop, we next examine how some sisters in those institutes describe what they see as the purpose of their governance structures and briefly examine their processes for restructuring their governance.

Governance Restructuring Process

Purpose of Governance

The governance structures of a religious institute are grounded in the vision and charism of their foundress/founder and initial members, and, not surprisingly, those initial structures are often reflective of the ecclesial, social, and economic context of their day. As the years go by and the ecclesial, social, and economic contexts change, so too do the underlying structures of how a religious institute practically governs itself.

Understanding what particular functions the institutes expect their governance structures to serve is key to better understanding what they hope to gain through restructuring. Generally speaking, there are three levels of governance in religious institutes, going from the most expansive to the most local. These sisters summarized it well:

> *We understand religious [institute] governance to be at three*
> *levels: general level: overseeing the unity of the [institute]; pro-*
> *vincial level: mission; local level: needs and care of the sisters.*
>
> *(1) General Governance Team: Promotes unity in international*
> *[institute]. (2) Province Leadership Team: Promotes vision and*
> *mission of the province. (3) Community Coordinators: Cares*

> *for the needs of the sisters locally, promotes charism and mission*
> *of each sister.*

As part of the same CARA/CommunityWorks, Inc., project, the leadership teams of religious institutes that were engaged in renewing their governance structures provided the purposes of governance as understood within each of their religious institutes, which were then grouped into the three broad categories.

Governance to Support the Institutes' Charism and Mission. Institutes reported that their governing structures exist to aid institute members at all levels in living out their charism and accomplishing the specifics of their mission. Leadership's good stewardship of the institute's resources, its management style, and its allocation of resources should provide practical support for the sisters' local ministerial needs, freeing sisters to focus mostly on their mission work. As two sisters responding to the survey put it:

> *The purpose of governance is to enable the whole body to discern the Mission of the [institute] according to changing circumstances and fidelity to the charism, and to help the sisters live this in their reality. It is to work toward the unity and cohesion of the body, while we are very dispersed. Governance also ensures initial and ongoing formation for the whole [institute].*

> *We believe that governance is in function of our mission, and our mission is in function to the needs of the world according to our charism. So, we agreed that we cannot embrace all the "priorities" that we already have in our circumscriptions—that we need to be more focused on our mission. Prioritizing will help us to expand our ministries to other places with urgent needs and to redesign our governance in a way that responds more appropriately to the challenges of today.*

All religious institutes—whether they are primarily in the United States and are experiencing decline or challenged by the inequality that has resulted from their dispersion on different continents—struggle with these issues:

- Institutes primarily in the United States that are declining in numbers are having to reinterpret their institute's charism and missions (such as education or health care) to better fit their reality of having few sisters actively engaging in ministries and a majority of their resources devoted to the well-being of their elderly sisters. In this instance, pulling younger sisters from active outside ministries to serve in leadership further exacerbates this situation.

- Institutes experiencing dispersion have also had to devote more resources to the care of their elderly sisters in the United States, while simultaneously having to adapt their charism and missions to the cultural contexts of the places where they still are experiencing growth. And often, with leadership positions disproportionately in the United States, the ability of those leaders to adequately understand the practical needs on the ground in another country are greatly diminished.

Governance to Exercise Authority Properly and Ensure Participation. In responding to the survey, sisters asserted that their governance structures should enable institute leaders to practice servant leadership by planning and working for the common good of the institute, with the leadership adequately representing and incorporating sisters of all countries, ethnicities, and cultures. Governance structures should allocate appropriate autonomy to all levels of leadership so that leaders have enough flexibility to respond to their locality's changing needs and situations. In addition, priority should be given to ensuring the participation of all sisters in institute life and promoting their shared responsibility.

Two sisters below describe their institute's goals with the redesign of their governance, the first wanting to make their institute's governance more flexible and localized, and the other wanting to rein in the autonomy of their institute's provinces:

> *The principle of subsidiarity. The decisions need to be taken at all levels (local, provincial, and general). Therefore, communication, dialogue, mutual trust, and respect of competence are needed.*

> *While there is an expectation that each provincial is accountable
> to the [institute] leader—there is a strong tendency to operate
> as independent "Queendoms." While we value and promote a
> circular model of leadership—the reality is we are very hierar-
> chical in structure.*

Again, how these purposes play out in the two kinds of institutes we sketched out in the two vignettes varies:

- Institutes that are primarily US based and are experiencing
  significant declines in their membership need their leaders
  to focus on the common good of the institute in light of the
  needs of their elderly members. In many cases, the leaders
  themselves are of advanced ages and these institutes struggle
  to have an adequate number of sisters to serve in their outside
  ministries and fill the institute's leadership positions.

- Those institutes experiencing growth in other countries, on
  the other hand, are challenged to have their governance structures proportionately reflect the number of sisters of different cultures, ethnicities, and countries. Leaders in another
  country are challenged to ensure that they are hearing from
  all sisters, particularly those actively engaged in ministries
  who are often spread out geographically.

*Governance for Caring for the Institute, Provinces, Communities,
and Sister Members.* The renewed structures need to promote unity
and cohesion at all levels of the institute, including between the
institute leadership and provincial leadership, among the provinces
and/or different regions, and among those of different ethnicities
or cultures. They need to promote and enable an engaged community life as well as provide for the sisters' physical, emotional,
and spiritual needs. It is important as well to foster growth in all
sisters through initial and ongoing formation.

The first of the two sisters below describes how governance
exists to help the members fulfill their institutes' mission. The
second discusses how they adjusted their governance so that it
better included members who do not serve in the United States.

> *In my mind, governance exists for the sake of service, and to support members to be who we are called to be and to do what we are called to do. It bears the responsibility for us to be faithful to the "requirements" of our active apostolic life together.*

> *During the process of reconfiguration almost all of our younger members coming from the South participated in the conversations with the aim of shaping the design of the new structure. However, historically, most of our members came from the North. At the beginning of the process our members from the South were few at the level of the leadership. Nowadays, their number is increasing and they are more involved in the decision making.*

Again, these issues of caring for the institute at all levels play out differently in the two kinds of institutes sketched in the two vignettes:

- For institutes with dwindling membership all in the United States, the struggle here is to adequately provide for elderly sisters' physical, emotional, and spiritual needs, sometimes at the expense of pulling resources from sisters in active ministries.

- Those institutes experiencing growth on another continent, on the other hand, struggle about where to place their resources. Their ministry needs on the other continents must be weighed against the need for resources to care for the elderly sisters in the United States. In addition, there is a tension between (a) centralizing decision-making authority to promote unity within an institute that has sisters of different cultures on multiple continents and (b) decentralizing decision-making authority so that adaptations can be made quickly for the local circumstances where sisters are currently ministering.

The Role of Institute Chapters in Changing Governance Structures
Some of the reasons that institutes must make decisions about their governance structures sooner rather than later are practical

ones. To change something as central to religious life as a governance structure requires a chapter meeting, a meeting of the institute attended by sister representatives from all branches of the institute. How representative that attendance needs to be varies by institute. For example, one that says that all active or semi-active vowed members must be in attendance would require almost all sisters, no matter what their age or continent of ministry, to congregate in one place, at which point the meeting is also greatly complicated by the logistical matters of entry visas for those in other countries and travel costs.

The Leadership Conference of Women Religious (LCWR), one of the two conferences of major superiors of women religious institutes in the United States, surveyed its member organizations to ask them to reflect on the specifics of their institutes' constitutions concerning chapter meetings and then to respond to two questions: (1) Does your institute have sufficient delegates to convene a chapter meeting now? (2) Will you have enough in the near future? The results, presented in figure 6.2, show the level of urgency in some institutes. While 86 percent of institutes say they currently have sufficient delegates for a chapter in the immediate future (within five years), that percentage drops to 28 percent concerning the near future (six to ten years). A majority (55%) say they are "not sure" they will have enough for the near future.

A related and equally time-sensitive question concerns whether each institute has sufficient members to serve in their current leadership structure should they hold an election at the chapter meetings. Again, the difference between how they responded about the immediate future and near future is instructive, shown in figure 6.3. While 80 percent say they have sufficient members for election in the immediate future, the percentage drops to 19 percent in the near future. Sixty-three percent report that they are "not sure" if they will have enough members for election in the near future.

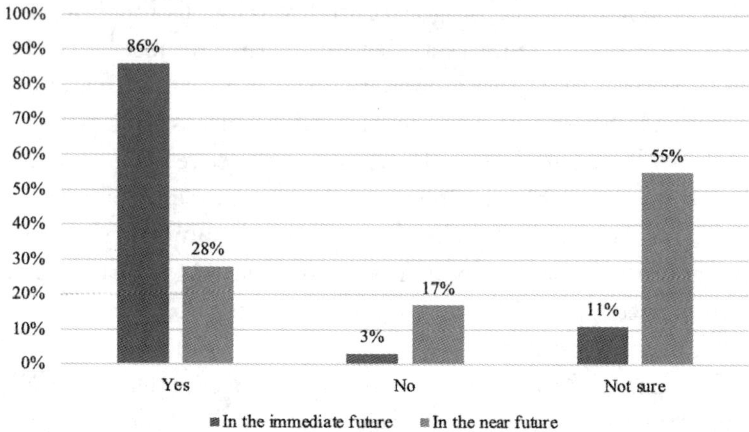

Figure 6.2. After considering the information on competencies for a chapter delegate, do you have sufficient delegates for a chapter? *Source:* Data from Thu T. Do, Jonathon L. Wiggins, and Thomas P. Gaunt, *Governance Structure: Survey of Members of the Leadership Conference of Women Religious* (Washington, DC: Center for Applied Research in the Apostolate, 2020).

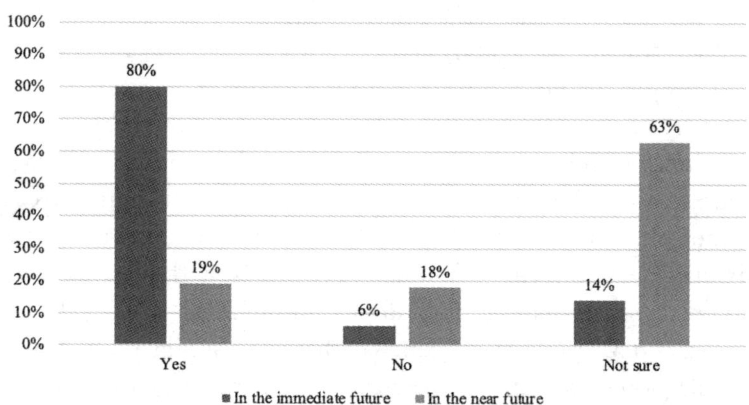

Figure 6.3. After considering the information on competencies for a chapter delegate, do you have sufficient members for election? *Source:* Data from Do, Wiggins, and Gaunt (2020).

Redesigning Governance Structures to Meet Current-Day Challenges

Religious institutes have creatively responded to the challenges they have encountered, something that would not be possible without some redesigning of their governance structures. Three of the most common challenges and the institutes' responses are presented below.

Meeting the Needs of Their Elderly Sisters While Remaining Focused on Their Mission as an Institute

Both of the types of institutes presented in the vignettes have the challenge of meeting the physical, emotional, and spiritual needs of their aging sisters. The challenges they encounter are best described by the two major superiors quoted below, which are taken from a 2021 CARA study of small aging women's institutes.[2] Faced with shrinking financial resources, escalating health costs, and wanting to keep the institute's members living in community as long as possible, these institutes have had to make some heartbreaking choices:

> *Probably the greatest tragedy that I experience as a prioress in challenges is that when my sisters—any one of my sisters—need more than one person to help them transfer; I have to move them to a nursing home. We can't afford to carry two people on our staff to do that care. So that is probably one of the most painful places that I have to go. Right now, we presently have two of our sisters in a nursing home through the [Institute Name] community here, so we're grateful. It's an excellent home, but we're separated from each other. With the Covid [pandemic], it has even been more difficult. So, I would say that's one of the greatest difficulties. The other one is that, with our dementia, which is only getting*

2. Jonathon L. Wiggins and Thomas P. Gaunt, *The Challenges Facing Small, Aging US Women's Religious Institutes with Limited Resources: Findings from the Focus Groups*, A CARA report (Washington, DC: Center for Applied Research in the Apostolate, 2021).

worse, we can't afford to hire somebody to come in and do projects with the sisters to keep them engaged. Some of our sisters do visit, and they walk with each other, and they have conversation at our table. But my sisters that have experienced more advanced dementia are pretty lost.

We also have a good number of sisters with dementia. We have been . . . we would love to have some type of self-contained unit for them, where people work directly with them, or people who have been trying to work with people with dementia, which we don't have. That's certainly lacking. Then, as both of you mentioned, kind of compounding this was Covid. We were fortunate that our sisters weren't confined to their rooms, but they were confined to a cohort with each other. Especially the sisters with dementia, when we eased those restrictions and then they were able to go back in a larger setting, they were very confused. So that has added to the confusion. We also have quite a large motherhouse. Just the size of the facility now is problematic for some of our sisters that aren't able to get around really well, and then to maneuver the space there. So those are some of the challenges that we have.

At the same time that they redirect institute funds and assign sisters to address the needs of their elderly sisters, the institutes want to remain focused on their mission, whether it be education, serving the poor and marginalized, or providing health care to the general public. The tension between the two can be a vicious cycle: pulling sisters from exterior ministries to care for the elderly sisters not only takes a sister away from a ministry but also reduces the funds coming in when she no longer earns a salary. This same phenomenon happens whether the institute is primarily US based or has been experiencing member growth outside of the United States.

Institutes' responses to this have been to reconfigure their governance structures so that fewer sisters are needed in leadership roles, freeing sisters to either take care of the elderly sisters or to be engaged in external ministries (whether they be in the

United States or in another country). Sisters from two of the institutes participating in the CARA/CommunityWorks, Inc., study describe their institutes' reasoning for making the governance changes below:

> *We previously have had four autonomous provinces in the United States with duplicates of leadership teams, secretariats, finance teams and now, as we become one province we can free many of those sisters for service in mission rather than confining them to province service.*

> *Hopefully it will enable some of our sisters formerly in leadership to minister more directly to our sisters and brothers in the world.*

This push-and-pull continues to be a challenge, however, even after the governance structures are redesigned to have fewer sisters in leadership. This will likely be the defining challenge facing US institutes in the coming decades.

Providing for the Needs of Sisters Ministering in Other Countries

With the headquarters of the institute often in the United States, sisters ministering in other countries sometimes feel that the decision makers do not necessarily understand the local contexts in which they are ministering. In addition, the US provinces of the institutes are often the ones with the most funds and infrastructure, with the foreign provinces struggling to provide ministries without the resources they need.

To address these issues, institutes have been redesigning their governance structures so that:

- more sisters from the Global South are involved in higher levels of institute leadership

- provinces have enough autonomy to make decisions regarding their local ministries without needing to get approval at the higher levels of leadership

- resources are shared more equitably among the provinces, regardless of where the resources originated

Some of the sisters give voice to these goals below, intentionally increasing their institutes' equity for provinces, subsidiarity, and interculturality:

> *Governance as stated in our Constitutions: "The purpose of our organizational structures is to free us to live our life of consecrated life for mission." Our structures should be flexible enough to respond to our lived experience and the changing world and needs of those who are the focus of our mission.*

> *The [Institute] Leadership Team feel they are far too removed from the lived reality of local Units/Provinces and therefore making decisions with insufficient information and local knowledge.*

> *In order to call forth leadership from the Global South we need to imagine more mobile teams.*

> *To uphold the unity of the [Institute] while honoring and promoting the richness of diversity, interculturality, and universality. We value subsidiarity, equality, and accountability at all levels and inclusion of our partners in mission.*

> *It was therefore difficult to feel the unity of the whole body. Each region was ploughing for itself. Difficult to make decisions that take into account the whole. For example, which houses to keep for which mission.*

Meeting the Financial Needs of Their Institute

Becoming more financially viable and being able to fund both the needs of their elderly sisters and their ministries is a continual challenge for many institutes. The default for many institutes is to have sisters fill the roles of treasurer and other financial positions, even though many of these sisters lack the expertise to fully reap the benefit of their assets or to plan well for the future. In addition, the financial and administrative positions are often duplicated in the provinces. A major superior from the 2021 CARA study of small aging women's institutes described the financial crises they face when trying to attend to the needs of their aging sisters.

> *We've given our life all over the [State] but we're not paid a just salary for a number of years. So, the financial piece of it weighs on us. It's that recognition that I trust . . . I mean we do have assets in our properties. At some point we'll have to sell those in order to take care of our sisters. But it's just a reality that we never received the income that would have been ours just for the parish work and the church schools that we taught in for a number of years.*

As the leader notes, part of getting their financial houses in order involves not only having more expertise in their staffs but also selling or remodeling their facilities. Below, three sisters from the CARA/CommunityWorks, Inc., study describe how they have addressed their financial challenges.

> *Our province was financially sustainable; one of the other three was not, so pooling resources would make it possible for all of us to be financially sustainable.*

> *There was a general lack of formation and information of the sisters about financial issues, which were dealt with by the superiors and bursars with no involvement of the sisters. A few sisters were qualified in administration, and they maintained their role for many years. There has not been a real handing over of this ministry over the years, with the preparation of a younger generation of sisters. A general, basic formation on financial issues has been missing.*

> *Realization that we could be more effective in mission if we combined resources (financial and human). . . . We are about five hundred members in the United States in four different provinces. . . . We are becoming one province.*

Summary and Conclusion

Facing tremendous challenges, one of the ways religious institutes are responding is through redesigning their governance structures. There is a sense of immediacy for some institutes as their sisters' median age is rising, they have more elderly sisters needing care than they have sisters in active mission-focused ministries, and there are fewer sisters able to serve in leadership. As the governance changes, they are creatively addressing those needs as well as those related to remaining mission-focused and becoming more financially stable.

The next chapter presents an overview of canonical considerations in the restructuring of governance in religious institutes. It describes the canonical issues that are involved in restructuring and presents some of the options that are available to institutes that are in these sorts of transitions.

Sharon Euart

Fidelity to the Journey
*Options for Canonical Restructuring
and Collaboration*

Introduction

Vatican II's Decree on the Renewal of Religious Life (*Perfectae Caritatis*) calls religious and the entire Church to an adaptation and renewal of religious life based on a return to the sources of all Christian life, especially the Gospel, as well as the original spirit of the founders and its adaptation to the changed conditions of our time (PC 2). Religious responded enthusiastically to the call to take a fresh look at their charism, spirit, purpose, and traditions and to adapt their proper law to new circumstances in the Church and the world. Particular attention was given to research and reflection on the spirit of the founder.

Thirty-one years after *Perfectae Caritatis*, John Paul II published the apostolic exhortation Consecrated Life (*Vita Consecrata*), inviting religious to view the future with hope and urging consecrated women and men to "look to the future, where the Spirit is sending you to do even greater things" (VC 110). Pope Francis, in the apostolic exhortation The Joy of the Gospel (*Evangelii Gaudium*), reiterates the words of Pope John Paul II: "All renewal in the Church must have mission as its goal if it is not to fall prey to a kind of ecclesial introversion" (EG 27). Pope Francis insists that personal conversion is not enough; religious institutes[1] are called to align their structures to the mission of the Church today. He urges religious in *New Wine in New Wineskins* "to not have fear of making changes according to law of the Gospel. . . . leave aside fleeting structures; they aren't necessary! And get new wineskins, those of the Gospel."[2] Today, while remaining steadfast in faith in Jesus Christ and in the joy and truth of the Gospel, religious institutes continue to respond to this call for renewal in ways and in light of signs perhaps not anticipated or even imagined fifty-five years ago.

Demographic Reality

Since the mid-1960s, the overall change in the demographics on women religious in the United States has been one of significant and persistent decline. From its peak of 181,421 in 1965 to 41,375 in 2020, this change represents a 77 percent decline.[3] The National Religious Retirement Office's 2019 Age Distribution data from 403 women's religious institutes indicate that 78 percent of the members are age seventy or above.[4] Half of the women religious in the United States are over age eighty.[5] But

1. Throughout this chapter "institute" will be used as the umbrella term for different types of institutes of consecrated life and societies of apostolic life described in canon law.

2. Congregation for Institutes of Consecrated Life and Societies of Apostolic Life, *New Wine in New Wineskins: The Consecrated Life and Its Ongoing Challenges since Vatican II* (Rome: Libreria Editrice Vaticana, 2017), no. 10.

3. See CARA, "Frequently Requested Church Statistics," http://cara.georgetown .edu/frequently-requested-church-statistics/.

4. National Religious Retirement Office, "Age Distribution of Religious," 4, https://www.usccb.org/offices/national-religious-retirement-office/statistics.

5. Stephanie Still, "Canonical Governance Options and Possibilities for Collaboration," *RCRI Bulletin* 24 (Winter 2020–2021): 4.

these statistics do not tell the full story. With a rising median age and a smaller number of new members, there are fewer sisters available for institute leadership and governance roles as well as for compensated ministry or external service. These signs correspond closely to the indicators of decline articulated in the apostolic letter Governing of the Holy Church (*Ecclesiae Sanctae*): "the small number of religious in proportion to the age of the institute or the monastery, the lack of candidates over a period of several years, the advanced age of the majority of its members" (ES 41).

In *Vita Consecrata*, Pope John Paul II also addresses the decrease in numbers of religious, "While individual Institutes have no claim to permanence, the consecrated life itself will continue to sustain among the faithful the response of love towards God and neighbor" (VC 63). He noted, however, that "it is necessary to distinguish the *historical destiny* of a specific Institute or form of consecrated life from the *ecclesial mission* of the consecrated life as such" (VC 63).

Today, religious life is in transition. Rather than a dramatic change, transitions usually manifest themselves gradually. Pope Francis referred to transitions during a Mass celebrated in Casa Santa Marta on October 23, 2015, "Times change and we Christians must constantly change. We must change steadfast in the faith of Jesus Christ, steadfast in the truth of the Gospel, but our approach must constantly move according to the signs of the times."[6] Addressing challenges and transitions in changing times in the Joy of the Gospel, Pope Francis urges consecrated persons to "be realists, but without losing our joy, our boldness and our hope-filled commitment" (EG 109). It is in this spirit of faith in Jesus Christ and the truth of the Gospel that this chapter will consider canonical options for restructuring the governance of institutes of women and men religious that are in transition and planning for a future of hope in fidelity to the journey.

6. Pope Francis, morning homily, Santa Marta, October 23, 2015, quoted in James V. Schall, "Pope Francis and the Changing Times," *The Catholic World Report*, November 13, 2015, https://www.catholicworldreport.com/2015/11/13/pope-francis-and-the-changing-times/.

Governance of Religious Institutes

When a religious institute is established, its proper law describes the institute's identity, founding charism, purpose, and traditions to be approved by an ecclesiastical authority to ensure that the institute will "flourish according to the spirit of the founder and sound traditions" (Code of Canon Law, c. 576). With this approval, the institute is given just autonomy for governing its internal life (c. 586§1) and for exercising the apostolate (c. 677§1).

Primary responsibility for sustaining the life and mission of the institute and protecting its identity rests with the superior general and the general chapter in accord with the institute's proper law (cc. 587§1, 622, 631). If the general government is unable to provide for the institute's life and the needs of its members as described in its proper law, the leadership of the institute must seek assistance in carrying out its responsibility to preserve the nature, spirit, and character of the institute according to the constitutions (c. 578) and the signs of the times.[7]

The response of institutes in the United States to the signs of the times has been and continues to be multifaceted. Some institutes have merged; others have combined provinces to create fewer and larger provinces or regions; still others suppressed provinces for a return to a centralized government as a single institute. Major superiors have been "recycled," serving first in the 1980s or 1990s and again in the 2000s; other major superiors are in third and fourth terms with indults from competent ecclesiastical authority. Some small institutes have formed "covenant relationships" with a larger institute to oversee administrative and management issues or look to other institutes to provide their canonical governance.

While the 1983 Code of Canon Law did not directly address the sharp decline in the number of vocations and the demographic

---

7. See Lynn Jarrell, "The Roles of the Religious Institute and the Diocesan Bishop When the Institute Is Facing the Reality of Decline," *CLSA Proceedings* 80 (2019): 174–94, for a detailed description of the responsibilities of the institute and the diocesan bishop.

shifts in the United States and other parts of the world, the law provides for mergers and unions of institutes, though these options are rarely used today and are no longer the preferred or ideal solutions. Today, institutes look for new options that will address canonical governance, the care of members, the institute's patrimony (c. 578), and its mission and legacy. What are some of the options for canonical restructuring?

Options for Restructuring in the Code of Canon Law

Several possibilities for restructuring religious institutes in the Code of Canon Law do not require permission from the Holy See for pontifical institutes or the diocesan bishop, in the case of a diocesan institute. There are, however, some forms of restructuring that require changes in the constitutions of the institute and subsequent approval by the Holy See or the diocesan bishop.

Division into Parts and Establishing New Parts

For example, canon 581 acknowledges the principle of subsidiarity in recognizing the proper authority of an institute (general chapter, supreme moderator, etc.) over the institute's internal structure. The canon describes the following actions: *Division into parts* occurs when a single institute is divided into provinces or regions, and *establishing new parts* is the creation of new units such as provinces or regions.

An example of institutes establishing new parts or creating new units is occurring in the United States when some international religious institutes mission small groups of members to establish a new community in the United States for a particular ministry.[8] Canonically, the group might be designated as a region, though

---

8. See *CARA Special Report on International Women Religious in the United States*, https://cara.georgetown.edu/Fall2019InternationalWomenReligious.pdf, for the results of a study on the experience of international women religious in the United States.

more frequently its canonical status is as a single community with a local superior accountable to the general superior in the home country. Prior to the arrival of the new community, the superior general has sought and received the written permission of the diocesan bishop where the community will reside. With this permission the members may exercise their ministry in accord with their mission and diocesan policy (c. 678§1).

Some of the new international communities eventually become diocesan institutes in the United States. Examples include the Lovers of the Holy Cross, which was founded in Vietnam in 1670. Following the fall of Saigon in 1975, many sisters left Vietnam and came to the United States. In 1992, a community of the Lovers of the Holy Cross was erected as a diocesan religious institute of the Archdiocese of Los Angeles.[9] The Sisters Adorers of the Holy Cross, a diocesan women's religious institute that was founded in Vietnam in 1670, began their ministry in the United States in 1979, and in 1995 a diocesan religious institute of the Archdiocese of Portland was erected in Oregon.[10] Many of the newly arrived international communities do not become diocesan institutes but over time become an important and integral part of the diocesan family. Most of these communities do not hold membership in either of the two religious conferences for women religious in the United States, the Leadership Conference of Women Religious and the Council of Major Superiors of Women Religious. They often affiliate with associations of international women religious around formation issues and similar cultural or ethnic experiences.[11]

9. See the Council of Major Superiors of Women Religious, https://cmswr .org/community/lovers-of-the-holy-cross-los-angeles/.

10. See the Council of Major Superiors of Women Religious, https://cmswr .org/community/sisters-adorers-of-the-holy-cross.

11. *CARA Special Report on International Women Religious in the United States*, 7, https://cara.georgetown.edu/Fall2019InternationalWomenReligious.pdf. Several of the international institutes are members of the Resource Center for Religious Institutes, which assists member institutes with financial, canonical, and civil law issues.

Small international communities also face legal issues after arriving in the United States. They often seek assistance with fundraising and tax exemption by asking to be included in *The Official Catholic Directory* (popularly known as the Kenedy Directory). The procedure is regulated by the United States Conference of Catholic Bishops (USCCB). In general, the process requires that any newly created, newly acquired, or newly affiliated Catholic nonprofit organization—such as an international community—seeking to qualify for exemption from federal income tax under section 501(c)(3) of the Internal Revenue Code through inclusion in the USCCB group ruling must file an application (Form 0928A) with the USCCB.

If the application is approved, the organization will be included in *The Official Catholic Directory* and recorded by the IRS in the Exempt Organizations Business Master File extract. The completed Form 0928A must first be approved by the general counsel of the local diocese where the international community is located, which then forwards the application to the USCCB. It is good practice to consult first with the general counsel or chancery office of the local diocese prior to beginning the process of completing the Form 0928A to avoid any unnecessary changes later in the application process. The USCCB has provided a link on its website that facilitates the process by listing the requirements and the forms to be completed. The links for the forms necessary for group inclusion in *The Official Catholic Directory* are found at the general counsel's page of the USCCB: https://www.usccb.org/www .usccb.org/offices/general-counsel/tax-and-group-ruling.

Other legal issues may arise as members of international institutes arrive in the United States, such as sponsor requirements, the integration and orientation of foreign-born religious into the American way of life, and adjustment to US immigration regulations. These concerns are of utmost importance to newly arrived religious, especially as they wish to obtain a driver's license, social security number, benefits, and other important documents. Resources to assist these institutes are available through various dioceses and the Religious Immigration Services at Catholic Legal

Immigration Network (CLINIC).[12] The *Guidelines for Receiving Pastoral Ministers in the United States, Third Edition* of the USCCB is also a helpful resource: https://www.usccb.org/sites/default/files /flipbooks/cclv-guidelines/cclv-guidelines/assets/basic-html /page-1.html#.

Mergers, Unions, and Federations

Canon 582 refers to mergers, unions, and federations of institutes of consecrated life and states that authorization for these forms of restructuring is reserved to the Holy See. A *merger (sometimes called a "fusion") of established parts* happens when an institute combines several units by modifying their composition, such as several regions becoming a province, the fusion of several provinces into a single province, or the consolidation of several provinces into a single institute. Other restructuring options are often referred to as a *merger* even though the structures and procedures for establishing them differ. A common example of a merger occurs when a small institute is absorbed into a larger institute. The effect of such a merger is that the smaller institute loses its proper identity and assumes the identity of the larger institute.

Another form of restructuring mentioned in canon 582 is creation of a *union or federation*, which occurs when several—two, three, or twenty—different institutes come together to form a new institute that is different from any of the individual institutes. An example of this option occurred when the Sisters of Mercy of the Americas was created in 1991. After ten years of planning, sixteen independent Mercy congregations and one union composed of nine provinces created a single institute with twenty-five provinces.[13] Referred to as the "Journey to Oneness," the institute

12. See Miguel Naranjo and Leya Speasmaker, "Integration and Orientation of Foreign-Born Religious," RCRI Webinar, November 2020, https://vimeo .com/541661172/a2421e7d95.

13. See Patricia McDermott, "Canonical Governance Options and Opportunities for Collaboration," *RCRI Bulletin* 24 (Winter 2020–2021): 8.

articulated a vision for the process in two questions: "Who do we desire to be for one another as Sisters of Mercy? Who do we desire to be for our suffering world?" Sister Patricia McDermott, RSM, president of the Sisters of Mercy of the Americas, said, "Vision is a must . . . and that vision must be about mission and life."[14]

Another example is the fusion of several provinces of the Society of Jesus in the United States to create the second largest Jesuit province: United States East. Regarding this reconfiguration, Reverend Arturo Sosa, SJ, superior general, said, "We are learning that Province reconfiguration helps us to recover our deepest identity as Jesuits. . . . [It] widens apostolic horizons . . . facilitating a more effective distribution of workers in the vineyard of the Lord."[15]

The conciliar and postconciliar documents *Perfectae Caritatis* and *Ecclesiae Sanctae* encouraged the merger of institutes and monasteries that, left alone, offered no reasonable hope for growth and development (*PC* 21–22; *ES* 39–41). If possible, such institutes were to be merged with institutes possessing a similar character, purpose, and spirituality and whose future looked more promising. The same was true for unions among institutes if, according to *Perfectae Caritatis* 22, "their constitutions and customs were practically the same and a kindred spirit animates them . . . especially when of themselves they are very small."[16] An important canonical requirement at the end of *Ecclesiae Sanctae* states that, prior to proceeding to a merger or union, every religious is to be heard and all is to be done in charity (*ES* 41).

14. McDermott, "Canonical Governance Options," 9.

15. See "Jesuits—USA East," https://www.jesuits.global/2020/07/27/birth-of-the-second-largest-jesuit-province-united-states-east-uea/.

16. See Sharon Holland, "New Institutes, Mergers, and Supression," in *Procedural Handbook for Institutes of Consecrated Life and Societies of Apostolic Life*, ed. Michael Joyce (Washington, DC: CLSA, 2001), 41–42, for procedures and options for individual members; Rose McDermott, "Institutes of Consecrated Life and Societies of Apostolic Life," in *New Commentary on the Code of Canon Law*, ed. John P. Beal, James A. Coriden, and Thomas J. Green (Mahwah, NJ: Paulist Press, 2000), 750–51.

Today, despite the availability of mergers and unions for re-structuring religious institutes, they are rarely considered practical options given the demographic realities of many institutes. The merging of two small institutes with few members and a high median age or a merger of several aging institutes only creates larger nonviable institutes. A primary concern of members of institutes regarding mergers and unions is a desire to maintain their identity and live their remaining years fulfilling their vocations as members of the institute they entered and to which they devoted their lives as religious.

Other Options for Canonical Governance for Institutes

Transitioning to Historical Fulfillment

Over the course of time, numerous religious institutes have ceased to exist for a variety of reasons. Similar to other social organizations, the life cycle of a religious institute begins, grows, expands, reaches maturity, declines, and dies or is revitalized as a new identity emerges.[17] Today, many religious institutes might be described as on a downward cycle, while others evidence a growth phase because of a new way of reimaging themselves.

Although most institutes in transition have been able to retain their canonical leadership, there is an increasing number of institutes that are moving toward fulfillment of their historical life

17. Amy Hereford, *Navigating Change: The Role of Law in the Life-Cycle of a Religious Institute* (St. Louis, MO: Religious Life Project, 2014), 99–103, and *Religious Life at the Crossroads* (Maryknoll, NY: Orbis Books, 2013), xiv–xvi. See also Lawrence Cada and Raymond Fitz, et al., *Shaping the Coming Age of Religious Life* (New York: Seabury Press, 1979), 12, in which the authors identify four phases in the life cycle of religious life: growth phase, decline phase, change-over phase, and growth phase under a new image. For another perspective, see Gerald Arbuckle, *Out of Chaos: Refounding Religious Congregations* (New York: Paulist Press, 1988). See also David J. Nygren and Miriam D. Ukeritis, *The Future of Religious Orders in the United States: Transformation and Commitment* ("FORUS") (Westport, CT: Praeger, 1993).

cycle and are in their final era of general government (namely, celebration of a general chapter and election of superior general and council) and no longer have members capable of exercising leadership roles. This can be a very painful time for an institute and its members. It also can be a time of peace and acceptance in which the members are sustained by the realization that they have responded faithfully to God's call and fulfilled the mission entrusted to them.

Though the process of moving toward historical fulfillment is not regulated in the Code of Canon Law, many of the following actions and procedures are guided by canonical principles.

Covenant Relationship

Canon 580 describes a relationship between religious institutes that respects the autonomy of each institute. The covenant relationship does not result in a merger of the institutes; rather, this relationship between the institutes has been described as a covenant or partnership to assist an institute coming to fulfillment on its journey. In recent years, there has been an interest in this type of arrangement. The covenant model, in which each institute retains its own identity, is contingent on the needs of the smaller institute and the resources of a stronger institute to meet those needs. Not all covenant relationships will be alike. Some may include providing oversight for financial administration, personnel services and property, provision for retirement and health care of members, administration of any remaining sponsored ministries, and legacy planning.[18]

The covenant relationship may be short term or long term, depending on the needs of the smaller, more fragile, institute.

---

18. See Amy Hereford, "CANON 580: Aggregation and Covenants," in Canon Law Society of America, *Roman Replies and CLSA Advisory Opinions 2012*, ed. Sharon A. Euart, John A. Alesandro, and Thomas J. Green (Washington, DC: CLSA, 2012), 83–86. See also "Planning for the Future: The Covenant Relationship," *RCRI News in Brief* 3, no. 4 (Fall 2011): 2–3.

When the smaller institute is no longer able to provide its own canonical governance, it might request leadership from outside the institute. This would require petitioning the Holy See or the diocesan bishop for a commissary or canonical trustee to provide canonical leadership during the last phase of the institute's journey.

Collaborative Governance Models

For some institutes moving toward historical completion, the covenant relationship is not the best option since it would only temporarily address the governance issues. It could also mean that the smaller, more fragile institute might be subsumed into the other, even though they are juridically separate institutes. Currently, there are two different models for collaborative governance implemented in US institutes.

In one model, the Sisters of the Most Precious Blood and the Franciscan Sisters of Mary began a conversation in 2013 and, after six years of intense planning, created a third civil corporation named Collaborative Governance (CG), which manages and oversees human resources, property management, legal issues, and management tasks for the institutes' remaining sponsored ministries. Each institute retains its own canonical governance for as long as possible. When it can no longer provide canonical leadership for the members of their respective institutes, each institute will petition for a commissary from the Holy See. The commissary could be selected from the members of the board of the new civil corporation, thereby providing a relationship between the two institutes that respects their heritage while providing the support necessary to live out their vocation. Sister Janice Bader, president of the Sisters of the Most Precious Blood, describes a significant advantage of this model as allowing the sisters "to maintain their identity as Sisters of the Most Precious Blood."[19] She also notes

19. Dan Stockman, "Collaborative Governance Model Helps Congregations Carry on with Limited Resources," *Global Sisters Report*, February 12, 2018. See Janice Bader, "Canonical Governance Options and Opportunities for Collaboration," *RCRI Bulletin* 24 (Winter 2020–2021): 11.

that openness and honesty are essential in collaborative ventures. "It is the only way to move from 'we/they' to 'us.'"[20]

A second type of collaborative governance model involving several religious institutes within a single geographic area is the Wisconsin Religious Collaborative (WRC), a small nonprofit corporation established in 2018. The collaborative is designed to serve member institutes of women religious "to enable greater stewardship of resources, facilitate collaboration in programs and activities, and support for personnel."[21] The leaders of nine religious institutes in Wisconsin and northern Illinois created mission and vision statements to focus the work of the collaborative. The members of the collaborative have different needs, and the institutes are at different stages of transition. An important step in the genesis of the collaborative was to connect or network with others experiencing similar challenges while sharing learning that can be helpful to other institutes through its website at www.WR Collaborative.org. The leadership of the collaborative believes that the time and energy invested in the effort is worthwhile and can result in "effective solutions, invigorating support and meaningful connections."[22]

Canonical Commissary

When an institute is moving toward historical fulfillment of its mission and is no longer able to provide for its canonical governance, it may petition the competent church authority for a canonical administrator or trustee, generally referred to as a commissary, who will be entrusted with the canonical governance of the institute. The process may begin when an institute is still able to elect a general superior/president but lacks members capable of serving as councilors. In this case, it is possible to seek a dispensation from the institute's constitutions to permit fewer councilors or

20. Bader, "Canonical Governance Options," 11.

21. See Lyn Korte, "Canonical Governance Options and Opportunities for Collaboration," *RCRI Bulletin* 24 (Winter 2020–2021): 13.

22. Korte, "Canonical Governance Options," 16.

for the appointment of a religious from another institute to serve as a member of the council. Although the latter solution has not been applied frequently, when it has, the experience generally has been positive for both the institute and the appointed councilor.

The appointment of a canonical commissary for institutes with no members able to serve in the general government is an alternative frequently considered today. Though it does not appear in the Code of Canon Law, this option is not new. The notion is that one person is providing oversight for others. The request for a commissary calls for serious prayer and discernment on the part of the requesting institute. Canonically, this involves derogation from the constitutions and proper law of the institute (c. 623).

A commissary is a person appointed by the competent ecclesiastical authority, either the Holy See for pontifical institutes or the diocesan bishop for diocesan institutes, with the canonical authority to act as the superior general/president for governance of the institute according to the constitutions and proper law of the institute the commissary is serving, as well as the decree of appointment.

Generally, a commissary for a women's institute is a woman religious with a similar experience of living religious life. Clerics can also be appointed, however, to serve in this role for women's institutes. Currently a layperson cannot be appointed a commissary for a religious institute. The requesting institute is encouraged to recommend a suitable person who is known to the institute to be appointed as commissary; however, the appointment of the commissary is made by the Holy See or the diocesan bishop.

As with every major superior, the commissary is to have a council (c. 627). If possible, all or at least some of the council members should be members of the institute she is serving. She can, however, ask assistance from members of her own institute. The councilors provide the collective wisdom needed for important decisions. In most cases, the commissary does not have a specific term (though a commissary could request one). The appointment is usually *ad nutum Sanctae Sedis* or at the will of the Holy See. The appointment may last several years, even throughout the lifetime of the last member of the institute.[23]

Together with the members of the institute, the commissary does what is necessary to plan for the closure of the institute when that time arrives. This would include first and foremost the care and well-being of the members, disposition of assets, ministries, and properties (if any remain) in accord with canon and civil law.

One leader of an institute in transition while also serving as a commissary for another institute describes the journey to historical completion this way: "Gratitude and Hope are sisters and we who journey to completion are challenged to bring Hope: To look forward with active hope; acknowledging our pain; letting go of what hinders us; viewing life with new eyes; moving forward to all God calls us to be."[24]

Summary and Conclusion

Today, leaders and members of religious institutes are all seeking the best way to move forward. Not everyone is prepared to face the realities of today and tomorrow. Those who have begun the work of restructuring for the future, as well as the latest research, urge others not to wait.[25] Now is the time. Members of institutes that are assessing options for restructuring canonical governance or moving toward fulfillment of their mission exude a spirit of

23. See "25 Q&As: Commissary for Religious Institutes," RCRI website at www .trcri.org, https://cdn.ymaws.com/www.trcri.org/resource/resmgr/2019_updates /commissary_q_and_a_2019_upda.pdf. See also Sharon A. Euart, "Canonical Governance: Commissary of a Religious Institute," in Canon Law Society of America, *Roman Replies and CLSA Advisory Opinions 2018*, ed. Sharon A. Euart and John A. Alesandro (Washington, DC: CLSA, 2018), 157–59.

24. Ann Lacour, "Canonical Governance Options and Opportunities for Collaboration," *RCRI Bulletin* 24 (Winter 2020–2021): 7.

25. See Sharon A. Euart, "Canonical Governance Options and Opportunities for Collaboration," *RCRI Bulletin* 24 (Winter 2020–2021). See also CARA 2019 Report to LCWR, August 2020.

faith, joy, and hope that continues to guide their mission and their lives. While this is a time filled with unanticipated challenges, it is also a time of spiritual growth and renewal as well as an occasion for strengthening communion through cooperation, joint efforts, and prayer.

In his homily on the World Day of Consecrated Life in 2018, Pope Francis offered an encounter with Jesus that can inspire all those in consecrated life. Francis spoke of the women before the tomb. They had gone to encounter the dead and their journey seemed useless. Pope Francis said, "You too are journeying against the current. . . . But like those women, keep moving forward, without worry about whatever heavy stones need to be removed. And like those women, be the first to meet the Lord, risen and alive. Cling to him and go off immediately to tell your brothers and sisters, your eyes gleaming with joy. In this way, you are the Church's perennial dawn."[26]

26. Pope Francis, homily, World Day for Consecrated Life, February 2, 2018, https://www.vatican.va/content/francesco/en/homilies/2018/documents/papa -francesco_20180202_omelia-vita-consacrata.html.

Patricia Cormack and
Maria Theotokos Adams

8

Experiences of Restructuring, Growth, Culture, and Ethnicity

As a number of religious institutes realistically address their diminishing number of members and creatively imagine how to come to completion, there are also new religious institutes that are inaugurating new missions in new countries. CARA invited Sister Patricia Cormack, SCSC, and Sister Maria Theotokos Adams, SSMV, to reflect on their experience in these two contexts. They were invited to reflect on the challenges of renewing governance from the experience of their community and how it applies more broadly to religious institutes in general. Their reflections are framed within these two questions: What excites you about religious life today? What worries you about religious life today?

Sister Patricia Cormack, SCSC

In 2004 and 2005, an idea surfaced on how to celebrate the fiftieth anniversary of the Leadership Conference of Women Religious (2006). From that idea came the traveling historical exhibit, "Women and Spirit," that outlined the contributions of women religious to American culture and history from the 1627 arrival of the first women religious in New Orleans. When the exhibit was decommissioned in 2012, a DVD was produced that captured the major themes of the exhibit.

If one spends time with the DVD, something unique about women religious in the United States becomes evident. The history of women religious in Europe, particularly from the Middle Ages to the colonial period, is a constant tale of charismatic ideas about an apostolic outreach by women religious that is forced eventually to return to strict enclosure as the only appropriate expression of the life for women.

This dynamic has shaped the way in which the organization and governance of congregations of women religious have developed over the years. The vision of what is or is not appropriate for religious life and, particularly, the life of women religious often circles back to some variation on this tug of war.

On the arrival of women religious in the Americas, the cultural and economic underpinning for enclosed religious life was nonexistent. Many of the religious who first arrived came through the invitation of bishops who needed a method for responding to pastoral needs. Sometimes, the original crisis that prompted the invitation had already been met (it took time to find willing volunteers and to travel to the Americas) or had evolved into something very different.

The genius that emerged from this development in the life of religious is the quick grasp of needs and the creative response to those needs. Survival often meant doing almost impossible tasks with little or no education or financial resources. Yet, these women succeeded. Leadership was born in the passion for mission and a fearless approach to life.

On many occasions, the women became a thorn in the side of church leaders who wanted to control how they worked and lived. But what emerged repeatedly were the innovations in education and health care that shaped the later systemic expression of those ministries. The solutions they developed were often unique and highly effective ministries that supported the development of Catholic pastoral life in a cultural environment that was not always welcoming.

Canonical governance developed in such a way that the ministries of the community could be carried out with as much flexibility as possible. This entrepreneurial spirit laid the foundations of the Catholic healthcare system and the Catholic educational system in the United States.

With the advent of the 1917 Code of Canon Law there developed a grudging recognition of forms of religious life suited to the apostolic dimension of ministry. Women religious worked with the canonical structures that forced a blending of a horarium more suited to enclosed contemplative religious and the demands of an active teaching or healthcare ministry. But for all that, the underlying question was always about the structure of governance that helped to make mission happen.

In the heady post–Vatican II days, we thought our efforts at renewal would make it all come round right. We experimented with an egalitarian view of community life. We were determined to treat each other as adults and to avoid any governance structures that reinforced a childish submission to authority in the name of obedience. We struggled to name the elements of our life together in service of mission. "What do we owe to each other in the process of serving the mission of the congregation?" "How do we collaborate to make that mission effective?"

As the period of experimentation closed and the special chapters designed to get us in touch with the roots of our charism concluded, we began a shift from institutional expressions of mission. At the same time, the reality of our situation as flawed humans became more evident. Our efforts at renewal would not make everything perfect.

We learned that individual efforts in ministry were harder to connect to the congregation. We learned that life as a witness to the following of Jesus was harder to articulate without an institutional expression. We learned that we must deal with our shadow side and the unhealed and unacknowledged hurts of our past (personal and communal) that unconsciously shape our choices and direction. Treating one another as adults and living out obedience to the mission was far more challenging than we expected.

The emergence of the Conference of Major Superiors of Women (CMSM) in 1956 facilitated the connections that would eventually result in the emergence of the Leadership Conference of Women Religious (LCWR). The frictions among women religious around the vision of leadership and governance weighed heavily.

Membership in LCWR was expanded to include all those in canonical religious leadership. Resistance to that movement eventually resulted in the recognition of a second body, the Council of Major Superiors of Women Religious, in the early 1990s by the Congregation for Institutes of Consecrated Life and Societies of Apostolic Life.

As ministerial presence in the Church developed, the later elaboration of institutional ministries, such as the emergence of healthcare systems, ministerial juridic persons, and the handing over of educational facilities to lay leadership came about. Women religious recognized the changes in their demographics that required a rethinking of leadership for their ministries. Many congregations were proactive in this to ensure the sustainability of their ministries.

In recent years, the Catholic Health Association (CHA) has presented a workshop on sponsorship prior to the LCWR annual assembly. In the 2018 workshop, a visual timeline of healthcare leadership was shared. This chart makes clear the planning and development of the gradual move from religious to lay leadership, then the development of healthcare systems sponsored by religious transitioning to canonically recognized sponsors of healthcare systems (Public Juridic Persons [PJP]).

In 1968, the chart lists 796 Catholic hospitals, either single or freestanding, all with a single sponsor (221 women religious sponsors and 4 men religious sponsors). All but 26 of the 796 hospitals were headed by religious. Twenty years later there were 616 Catholic hospitals; 444 of them were within 60 Catholic healthcare systems. Of the 616 hospitals, only 196 were headed by religious. Six of the 60 Catholic systems were a PJP or similar sponsorship models. In 2018, there were 654 Catholic hospitals, 557 of them in Catholic systems. All of the 654 hospitals were headed by laypersons. Twenty of the 44 Catholic systems were a PJP or similar sponsorship models.

In more recent years, the attendees at the CHA sponsorship workshop have included leaders in Catholic education interested in developing similar types of leadership structures for Catholic schools sponsored by religious.

Today the hard lessons of the early years are no less pertinent. Reflection on present needs continues to tap into the charismatic and the prophetic dimensions of the life. It is as though there is a constant undercurrent of assessing needs and creating unique responses to those needs. This approach is akin to the DNA of the life in the USA.

My own community is a good example of this expression. In some ways, we are a "later generation" of religious life in the United States, since we arrived long after many of the congregations who were first established in the years before and immediately after the founding of the nation.

We were founded in Switzerland in 1856 by a Swiss Capuchin friar who was a pioneer in the social and educational services during a time of anti-Catholic bias in Switzerland. We carry on his insight that "the need of the times is the will of God." Our beginnings in the United States came in 1912 at the request of the bishop of Bismarck, North Dakota (a Swiss Benedictine). He wanted a hospital in Dickinson, and he tried to enlist various congregations without success. His claim on us succeeded because he had three blood sisters who were members of the community, and he was not above sitting on the doorstep of the motherhouse until he got a favorable response.

The year 1912 was a difficult time for German-speaking Swiss, German, and Austrian sisters to adjust and to cope with the mistrust of citizens of a country eventually to be at war with the

Austro-Hungarian Empire. Yet within eleven years we were staffing three hospitals (North Dakota, Illinois, and Wisconsin) and teaching in a two-room "boarding school" in the midst of the wheat fields of North Dakota. In each case, we started from scratch, and patients or students ate first.

Eventually, we were engaged around the country in other parochial schools and catechetical ministries, almost all of them in small towns in rural "mission" dioceses. They were spread out across many states, so our local communities were usually quite small—two or three sisters. The hospitals needed more sisters, but never beyond twenty-five. Until Vatican II, the bulk of our vocations (two or three a year) came from contact with students or workers in our hospitals. As was the case with most of the religious in those years, mission came first and education followed gradually. A sister did what was needed where she was stationed. The key question was, "How can we make this work?" We trusted that the resources would follow.

The Sister Formation Conference and the wisdom of congregational leaders intent on the professional development of young sisters marked a shift necessitated by the growing attention to proper credentialing. Salaries did not always match that necessity.

The Second Vatican Council led to a move from our institutional expressions of mission to the very creative one-on-one expansions into mission effectiveness, social service, parochial or diocesan ministries. The more traditional institutionally based ministries were not less valued, but they no longer needed our entrepreneurial energy. Now, the need of the times pushed us to ministries inside and outside of Catholic circles. Our governance structures evolved to enhance the new efforts. Provincial chapters focused more and more on organizational planning. We moved to a form of election of provincial leadership with affirmation by our general leadership.

Our experience mirrored the trajectory of many congregations in the United States. Vatican II's appreciation of the baptismal charism opened the ministerial agenda to a much wider expansion of forms of service and persons to carry that out. Social justice concerns urged the development of organizations like Network, a Catholic lobby for social justice that was begun by women religious and now reflects a partnership with laity that is quickly moving to lay leadership of the whole enterprise. The success of "Nuns and Nones" groups reflects the shared vision of respect for others and creative outreach to those in need. The Resource Center for Religious Institutes also has its roots in the legal desk at both LCWR and CMSM as well as the National Association of Treasurers of Religious Institutes.

In more recent years, we are seeing a decline in our membership but also a willingness to continue reaching out. Crises are still prompting creativity and an uncanny ability to network and organize with whatever we have to give. "There has to be a way to make this work!"

Witness the fundraising efforts of LCWR to support the ministries of the sisters of New Orleans following Hurricane Katrina. While the USCCB rightly focused on supporting the schools and parishes devastated by the storm, women religious organized and networked with Catholic donors to raise $7.1 million for the devastated ministries and motherhouses of religious.

More recently, the efforts of women religious at the southern US border have called on volunteers and donations from religious communities to meet critical needs. The instinct to step up and step in to collaborate and network together is still powerful despite the aging ranks of many communities.

It is clear that there will always be needs that require creative and unique responses. This is how God has called religious over the centuries. That call will continue. We don't know what that will look like, where God will lead it, but we do believe that God calls and waits for a generous response.

We know that neither my community nor other communities are guaranteed eternal existence. But it does mean that the spirit will inspire those who can form new communities to respond to new needs going forward. The grace we need now is to nurture the call and allow new forms of the life to surface. I like to think of us as quality compost for the future! God plants the seeds and makes them grow wherever and however God wants it to be. This is what gives me hope for the life.

More recent developments in governance models are still in their infancy. Many communities have considered merger with others, covenanting with others, and, even more recently, structured collaboration to support the internal management and governance needs of communities.

The mergers of communities developed in two parallel ways. Some of the larger congregations in the United States have either moved to merge provinces in a specific region or united all provinces into a single general governance model. Examples of these are the seven provinces of Mercy Sisters merged into a single community under a general leadership team. Both of the School Sisters of Notre Dame provinces in Canada, Chicago, and the East Coast merged into the Atlantic Midwest Province, and four provinces in Minnesota, Wisconsin, Missouri, and Texas merged into the Central Pacific Province.

The other type of merger has been the joining together of smaller communities of the same charism into a single congregation. This was the case for seven St. Joseph Sister communities that joined together as the Congregation of St Joseph. Similarly, seven Dominican communities banded together to form the Dominican Sisters of Peace.

In 2017, the LCWR Region 9 Collaborative Project researchers sought out ten communities with different types of covenant or one-to-one collaborative relationships in order to learn from them. Some of the observations that surfaced are as follows: collaborative relationships often emerge where there has been either previous formation or previous ministry experiences shared in common, some geographic proximity is inherent in the collaborative relationship, and the smaller communities in the collaborative relationship were financially stable and were expected to remain so. Generally, economic factors were not a reason to seek collaborative relationships; rather, a concern about leadership for the future as well as management of resources were reasons. Some communities began planning twenty years ago for collaborations that have not yet been fully implemented but will be in the near future.

As the twenty-first century moves along, we find ourselves at a crossroads. The practices and policies of the recent past have served us well but are no longer sustainable. "There has to be another way to do this." Conversations among leaders are focusing more and more on how to hand on our legacy and how to collaborate with one another. For women religious in LCWR Region 9, this was the thought that resulted in the development of the Wisconsin Religious Collaborative.

Nine congregations have banded together to create an organization capable of supporting the internal governance and management of member congregations. Being willing to try new ways, to learn from mistakes, and to work together to create new practices and policies that can sustain the life have been the key to this exploration. The outcomes are neither completely foreseen nor guaranteed for success. The effort is organic and unfolds daily. But the theme is the same. We have needs and we can create new possibilities.

The collaborative was incorporated in spring 2018 and the first executive director was hired in January 2019. During the last two and a half years, the organizational infrastructure was established, two series of needs assessment were conducted and focus areas were identified for development. Each area has an advisory committee consisting of professionals and religious institute members. Together with the executive director, specific plans of action have been or are being developed (see figure 8.1).

Early efforts have resulted in a series of roundtable sessions for information technology. These have allowed member institutes and their staff members to access experts in IT. A five-session virtual retreat was made available as part of the work of ongoing formation. Initial steps in identifying "preferred vendors" in financial management and human resource management have been developed. The vendors are vetted by the executive director and advisory committee members and offer appropriate discounts or some extra services at no cost.

In 2021, three service areas are receiving top focus. Planning for

- the disposition of archival materials for institutes moving toward completion of mission

- collaboration in providing social justice resources and support for communities without staff members to accomplish this

- exploration of ways that institutes can identify and access mental health resources and services

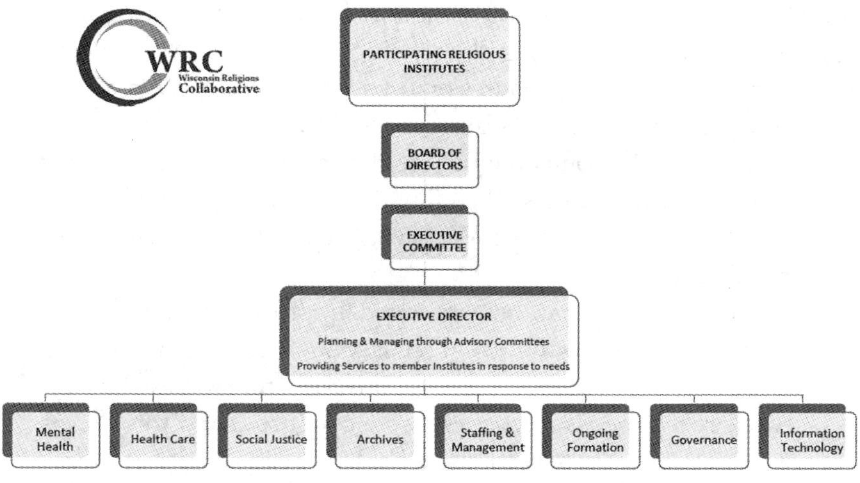

Figure 8.1. Organizational structure of the Wisconsin Religious Collaborative.

The Wisconsin Religious Collaborative will continue to develop and support religious institutes in the region.

Now as we look to the future, the biggest challenge for many leaders is to help community members recognize the need for changes at a time in life where stability in structure is their desire. Stability is not, however, guaranteed. Fostering hope, allowing the direction and vision of the life to emerge, acknowledging what can no longer sustain us, having the courage to step out into the unknown, relying on the grace of the Spirit and not fearing mistakes are all part of leadership now.

Finding the wherewithal to do all this takes the connection and encouragement of others in the same position. We are not alone, and this too is a grace of the development of governance structures that still have the age-old goal of making ministry happen. This too is a response to the need of the times.

Sister Maria Theotokos Adams, SSVM

Introduction

Because early Church history is the topic of my own academic research, I am especially aware that we are all a part of "contemporary Church history" in the making. Religious life has a particular presence in the Church that points to the legacy of the past as well as to the future. The present opportunity to contribute to this CARA publication allows me to become a "voiced subject" within a field of sociological analysis. While reflecting on my own experiences as a third-millennium vocation in a new international missionary congregation, I will also share the concerns and the great hope I have for the future of consecrated life in the Church at large. But in order to go beyond the statistics alone, I will first have to take my place in the dataset, then describe what my lived experience has been like, and finally lay out the larger view I see from here.

Taking My Place in the Dataset

My parents were Baby Boomers, both of my grandfathers were career military officers, and each of my privileged grandmothers excelled in various strengths and weaknesses (one could cook, but never learned to drive; the other drove, but never cooked). Arriving in the blizzard of 1978, I was the only child born to my parents. I received infant baptism from a Jesuit at Georgetown but did not receive any subsequent Catholic education. I grew up going to Sunday Mass in the Catholic Church with my young divorcée mother during the school year. In the summertime, I attended weekly services in the Episcopal Church presided by my father, an Episcopal priest and an occasional architect and boat designer on the side. After a very good prep school education, a gap year travelling abroad in French monasteries, and an Ivy League degree in ancient studies, I entered religious life in 2001, exactly one month after graduating from college. It seemed perfectly clear to me at that time that there was simply nothing better to do with my life than to spend it all on Jesus, who had unexpectedly become my greatest love.

I professed my perpetual vows in our congregation, the Institute of the Servants of the Lord and the Virgin of Matará (SSVM), in October 2008 alongside my novitiate and juniorate classmates: a Mexican sister who had been working in Delaware before entrance, a Colombian sister who had first met our community in Canada, and three other Anglophone American sisters (two from Maryland, one from Pennsylvania). At the time we all entered our community in 2001, there were only two American sisters out of 350. Today, there are over 150 American sisters out of 1,350 worldwide—some still in formation, many serving in the United States, some in our contemplative branch, and a good number in the foreign missions.[1] In some ways, much has changed in just twenty years. But in other ways, we simply keep working and praying and seeking to know and do God's will; before you realize it, you are building your congregational history.

Sharing What My Lived Experience Has Been Like

Although my experience of being an American entering a foreign missionary religious institute did technically make me the "Caucasian English-speaking minority," I never felt like a great

---

1. At the time of this writing, there are American sisters missioning in Canada, Guyana, Papua New Guinea, Taiwan, the Philippines, Tanzania, Egypt, Lithuania, Iceland, Ireland, the Netherlands, Belgium, Luxembourg, France, Spain, and Italy.

burden or a shocking oddity. When one is new to religious life, everything is new! The United States was simply one more mission territory, and we were one more example of "local vocations" from the foreign missions. It helped that three of us met our sisters abroad and so understood our vocations from the start within the missionary dimension and its international character. The Argentinian sisters who were our formators and first superiors were committed missionaries who had worked hard to learn English very well and to study American culture. They also understood that here, as in all the foreign missions, bringing the Gospel meant strengthening the life of faith in parishes and in families. Wherever the Christian life is thriving, some of the faithful will experience the call from God to deepen their baptismal promises by joining the consecrated life. Fostering vocations—whether to our institute or to other congregations—is a natural dimension of missionary work. As a missionary in a missionary religious institute I quite naturally learned Spanish and discovered in a new way the immigrant experience of my own country. Here are a few facts about my other "family profile."

Our institute was founded in 1988 by Father Carols Miguel Buela (b. 1941) as the female branch of the Religious Family of the Incarnate Word, a religious family composed of the religious priests and brothers of the Institute of the Incarnate Word (IVE, 1984) and the lay members of the Third Order Secular. The first sisters gathered at the foot of the Andes Mountains in San Rafael, Argentina, not far from where the IVE seminary had been founded a few years earlier. Shortly after the foundation, many young women from the local agricultural zone as well as from the metropolis of Buenos Aires and other major cities traveled to San Rafael to join the sisters. Attracted by our missionary charism to "prolong the incarnation" through the evangelization of the culture, these first sisters hoped to give their lives entirely to Christ and to the missions of the Church as consecrated religious, understood to be first and foremost *sponsa Christi*, "spouse of Christ." I believe that we shared in a particular moment of 1980's Catholic youth culture that became unexpectedly open to the religious vocation, despite the widespread trends away from religious life in the 1970s. These circles were commonly marked by a sudden enthusiasm to combine the teachings of the Second Vatican Council within a hermeneutic of continuity and to respond to the appeal that Pope John Paul II was making to the youth of the world to become great saints of the third millennium.[2]

In the early 1990s, when the first missionary foundations appeared outside of Argentina (in Peru, Paraguay, and Brazil), a few unexpected vocations arrived from Europe and the United States. Young women who had met the IVE missionary priests working in Rome and in New York found holiness in their way of life, charism, and particular manner of living the evangelical counsels. Some travelled all the way to Argentina to enter the Institute. What did these first Italian, Dutch, and US "Yankee" and US Caribbean sisters find in the humble *Convento de San José* in a dusty little town in South America? What unexpected cultural exchange and language difficulties mixed in their hearts with the enthusiasm of postulancy, novitiate, and first profession?

The mid-1990s marked a very important period for our congregation with the establishment of many new foundations outside of Argentina: Bethlehem (Holy Land), Kazan (Russia), Sezze (Italy), New York (United States), Taipei (Taiwan). These years also saw the establishment of houses of formation to receive vocations in Peru and Brazil. At the same time, the worldwide spiritual preparation for the Great Jubilee of the Year 2000 corresponded intimately with our charism to prolong the incarnation in all au-

---

2. The second World Youth Day took place in Buenos Aires, Argentina, in April 1987. Many of our first seminarians and sisters participated in this event as laypeople and were influenced by the renewal of youth ministry the pope's visit brought about. Fr. Buela, our founder, had been closely following the writings, travels, and historic actions of the Polish pope since his election in 1978. After the Bible, the Code of Canon Law, and the documents of the Second Vatican Council, the single most-cited authority in our Constitutions and Directory of Spirituality is Saint John Paul II.

thentic manifestations of culture. The pontificate of John Paul II and the fall of Communism invited us to rebuild the Christian faith in the territories in the former Soviet republics. Over the next fifteen years we opened missions in Ukraine, Tajikistan, Albania, and Lithuania. At the same time, new foundations opened in Ecuador, Chile, Hong Kong, the Philippines, and Papua New Guinea as well as expansions in other countries. The United States opened a novitiate in 1998 and a juniorate house of studies in 2001. Because we understand ourselves as foundationally missionary, always open to the "other," we naturally respect authentic diversity among international vocations while always finding unity in Christ.

This respect for cultural and ethnic diversity comes easily to an order originating in the New World, specifically in Argentina. Among the countries of South America, Argentina most properly should share with the United States the name of "melting pot." Early in the country's history, the first Spanish colonists included the missionaries who brought the Gospel to the tribe of Matará. In 1594, an indigenous artist from the tribe of Matará carved an illustrated catechetical teaching cross in mistol wood (from the "Argentinian jujube") reflecting his own artistic sensibilities and indigenous cultural expression. This artifact, known as the Cross of Matará, stands out as an eloquent witness to the spirit of "evangelization of culture." We wear replica Crosses of Matará as part of our religious habit, and our name Servants of "the Lord and the Virgin of Matará" refers to the carved Jesus and Mary found on this cross.

Argentina's history, however, not only arises from the indigenous and Spanish foundations but also includes more recent waves of immigrants from other parts of Europe and the Middle East. In addition to German, Swiss, Welsh, and French settlers, the "Avellaneda Laws" of the late nineteenth century spurred a huge wave of fresh Italian and Spanish immigration to Argentina, which lasted well into the twentieth century. The very large influx of Ukrainians, Lebanese, and Syrian Christians in the early twentieth century further diversified the ethnic, cultural, and liturgical mix.[3] Many of our members not only have indigenous-Spanish ancestry but also know about the immigrant experience of their grandparents or great-grandparents, including those whose own mothers or fathers emigrated because of the Spanish Civil War or World War II. Pope Francis, himself an Argentinian with an Italian-born father, is only the best-known example of many such multiethnic mixings. The Italian "barrios" of Buenos Aires where Bergoglio grew up resemble the sprawling "Little Italy" neighborhoods of Brooklyn or the Polish enclaves of Chicago. Growing up in such places, one learns from an early age how different people can live and work together, and that prepares the ground for recognizing the unique bonds of unity that only Christ can forge between peoples.

Even before experiencing the interface with Latino culture in my consecrated life, I learned much from Asian culture. The novitiate class ahead of me was composed of Filipina sisters who had nearly all discerned their vocations with our missionary priests while working in Hong Kong to support their families back in the Philippines. These new women religious (mostly in their thirties) were well versed in prayer, sacrifice, hard work, joy, and service. They all spoke perfect English, but under duress or for discretion they would suddenly lapse into Tagalog or Ilocano. Three of us Americans had arrived at the convent directly from completing our undergraduate educations, but we learned many real lessons from our "older sisters," who knew how to do all the things we didn't (like cooking for twenty people with whatever limited ingredients were at hand, and ironing habits with speed and precision) and who had a plethora of virtues we lacked (like heroic cheerfulness and deep

---

3. Argentina has historically had some of the largest communities of Ukrainian Byzantine Rite Catholics in South America, as well as Chaldean and Maronite Rite Catholics. The presence of these non-Latin rites was most robust closest to the time of initial immigration when language and culture bonded each group together most strongly.

faith in God's Divine Providence, even in the face of unpromising conditions). I have often thought that the poem "Girl" (1978) by Jamaica Kincaid gives a litany of the kinds of maternal information they gave us—but without the condescension or oppression. "This is how to sew on a button; this is how to make a buttonhole for the button you have just sewed on; this is how to hem a dress when you see the hem coming down. . . ." After all, many of them had been nannies and they knew how to gently coax, instruct, and guide the helpless and the hapless with exquisite charity.

The diversity of our experience and character confers many blessings and has deeply enriched my faith. During my novitiate and juniorate period in the Hispanic ministry of Washington, DC, I met the newest immigrants from Mexico and Central America. One Advent season during my time in formation we participated faithfully in several long nights of neighborhood *Posadas*—Christmas caroling with two parishioners dressed up as Joseph and Mary reenacting their search for a home that will take them in. When the final refrain begins, the doors are thrown open with the lines: *Entren, Santos Peregrinos, Peregrinos, reciban este rincón, que aunque es pobre la morada, la morada, os la doy de corazón!* ("Enter now, Holy Pilgrims, receive this little corner, for although it is a poor dwelling, I give it with all my heart!") Then we all entered a humble, often crowded, apartment full of great joy and hospitality. Family members posed for their picture with "Joseph" and "Mary" as a sign of their welcome to the Baby Jesus who was denied a place in Bethlehem. I was always touched by the kindness and generosity of these families who were not accustomed to having White Americans in their homes but who eagerly shared with us the brightly colored Mexican breads and cups of hot thick *horchata*. After all, we were not there *as Americans* but as sisters within a congregation of sisters who did speak Spanish and who served the community—missionaries from a missionary order who were also ready to put aside our own ways to experience their language, culture, and devotional practices within the one common home of the Catholic Church.

Describing the Larger View from Here

The challenges and hopes for religious life in the United States today are both complex and simple, as the research presented here has shown. Religious life faces the difficulties of aging systems, a call for restructuring, the challenges of diversity, a need for evangelization, the lack of vocations, and a skeptical malaise in the secular culture at large. *Why be a sister? A religious brother? Why even believe in God at all?* But the solution is as simple as it ever was: Jesus.

My main worries for the future of religious life are actually tied to the anthropological crises of technology and family deterioration. I don't doubt that God will continue to call souls to consecrated life, but I worry that high doses of "screen time" and social media will adversely affect their capacity to receive the contingent graces. Young people who have grown up surrounded by constant digital communication may find it much harder to discover and to respond to the religious vocation. Formation programs may have to commit a lot more time and creativity to human formation than was necessary in the past. We are only beginning to understand the impact of digital addiction and of online personality development of the human person. *If someone's concentration is shot, how much harder is it for them to learn how to pray well? If someone's entire education has taken place superficially scanning digital texts, how can we teach them* lectio divina? *If the "answers" all come from quick Google searches, how can we prepare them to think and to read thoughtfully and deeply?*

Similarly, I worry that the breakdown and "restructuring" of families threatens to undermine the development of natural virtues important for religious life. Human maturity is forged in the home from childhood through adolescence. Confidence and humility are natural virtues that dispose a young woman to want to keep growing and to receive corrections while still knowing "who she is." *If a young woman has never been accustomed to family meals seated at the table, how will she adjust to community life and making herself known and understood?* Authentic sexual maturity and chastity can be eroded in families that are fractured by divorce, remarriage, or the example of "parental dating." *If no bond of love seems to last for long, how much harder will it be to imagine persevering in one's vows all the way to the end?*

I also acknowledge that the old model of the parish school and its attendant convent is coming to an end in many places. Real estate pressures and empty buildings combine to see the end of a kind of nineteenth- and twentieth-century heyday in American Catholic religious life. These changes are especially painful for those who remember how it was and who have to oversee the logistics of divesting themselves of their congregational goods. Also, I understand that many congregations face demographic realities that will eventually result in the end of their institutes. While this too must provoke a sense of critical urgency and anxiety, we should remember that these moments do not signal the end of religious life itself. No particular congregation has been granted indefectibility; only the Church has.

Some ancient religious orders have endured through great times of trial and rebirth. But many others have completed their mission and ceased to exist in the pilgrim Church in time. The founders, the charism, the members, and those souls they served, however, continue to live forever before the face of God, in the Heavenly Church, the true Zion that will never pass away. And in every age the Holy Spirit has called forth founders to establish new ways of living out the evangelical counsels. I don't doubt that he will continue to do so.

Above all, I remain joyful and hopeful concerning the future of religious life because Jesus is God and he is forever calling souls to himself. Nothing can stop his love or his power to attract young people to this way of life. The particular manifestations of religious life may change to a certain degree, but the essential elements of his way of life cannot: poor with Christ poor, chaste with Christ chaste, obedient with Christ obedient—*even unto death, death on a cross*. Consecrated life is a gift of the Trinity, so it cannot be reduced to a narrow experience of one place or another, of one historical situation or another, of one cultural or ethnic profile or another.[4] The radical love of Christ will always galvanize heroic

---

4. John Paul II, postsynodal exhortation *Vita Consecrata* (1996), "Chapter 1: *Confessio trinitatis*, The Origins of the Consecrated Life in the Mystery of Christ and of the Trinity" (14–40), especially paragraphs 21–22.

young people to leave all and to follow him. And in times of adversity religious life becomes more obviously and importantly prophetic. Where there is no interest or cultural hospitality, continue to proclaim the Gospel through the simplicity of community life and the faithful witness of charity and service to Christ in the least of our brothers and sisters. Where there is persecution, set up a convent in an apartment together and make the back bedroom into a chapel. If there are lots of vocations and no space to put them, build bunkbeds. If stipends dry up and benefactors become uninterested, go begging and trust in God. If the world hates you . . . *remember it hated me first, there is no servant above his master.* Religious life has always had a bright future in the midst of extreme difficulties because it is then that it is closest to imitating Jesus Christ, the Bridegroom of our souls.

Summary and Conclusion

Sister Patricia and Sister Maria Theotokos share their different experiences of religious life today from the perspectives of an older established religious institute and a new religious institute only recently established in the United States. Sister Patricia speaks to the challenges of an aging and diminishing institute and the creative efforts to address that reality in a collaborative and positive manner. Sister Maria Theotokos expresses the enthusiasm of a new and growing institute attentive to the challenges of the twenty-first century. Referencing Saint John Paul II, she writes: "Consecrated life is a gift of the Trinity, so it cannot be reduced to a narrow experience of one place or another, of one historical situation or another, of one cultural or ethnic profile or another." In the next chapter we lay out some of the learnings that we have gleaned from these pages, in hopes that they will provide fruit for reflection and ideas for renewal.

What Are We Learning?

Thomas P. Gaunt

The life and ministry of women religious have changed dramatically in the United States and across the world. This is not new, as previous generations of sisters have also experienced similar changes as they addressed the challenges of their time and place. What are we learning as we research the changes of the past twenty years or so? This final chapter summarizes key learnings about who the newer women religious are and the ways they are shaping the future of religious life. We have also observed how the leadership and structures of religious life are evolving to better address the great changes that have occurred or will be occurring in the Church and society.

Who Are the New Women Religious?

The ethnic and cultural diversity of the Catholic community in the United States has increased over the past fifty years and the newer members of religious institutes reflect this, though they are often entering religious institutes that have been overwhelmingly

White European in membership. Many of the newer members are immigrants or the children of immigrants, coming from families where devotional practices and family religious engagement are more common than in nonimmigrant families. The cultural or familial dimension of Catholicism is a strong factor in their vocation to religious life.

In recent years, religious institutes have begun to recognize the importance and value of developing intercultural and intergenerational communities. These efforts are ongoing and challenging as the two characteristics (diverse cultures and diverse generations) often go hand in hand. The older generations (those over sixty) are overwhelmingly White European and greatly outnumber the younger generation (those under sixty), who are more significantly from Hispanic, Asian, and African families.

The research presented here illustrates some of the particular challenges of sisters who are the only members of their ethnic or cultural group in their community or institute. Sisters speak of not being understood and of the experience of isolation within their religious community. Notably, newer sisters see that there is still much work to be done to authentically embrace a diversity of cultures and confront racism within their institutes.

Another group of new women religious are those sisters ministering and studying in the United States but who belong to an institute whose motherhouse and leadership is outside of the United States. These "international sisters" are initiating new ministries and communities across the country with sisters far younger than their US counterparts and bringing the richness of their institute's charism (from countries such as Vietnam or Nigeria or India or Argentina) to share with others.

The newer women religious, therefore, include not only those born and raised in the United States but also immigrants and missionaries to the United States. The reality of "who" newer sisters are is quite a contrast to our common popular images and stereotypes. They bring a new richness of diversity in culture, ethnicity, and religious customs that add color and vitality to religious life.

How Are the Leadership and Governing Structures of Religious Life Evolving?

Most religious institutes of women in the United States are challenged by the demographic reality of their membership, as two-thirds or more of their members are elderly or infirm. This reality limits the number of sisters who are in full-time active ministry or available for leadership roles in their institutes. This reality also challenges the institute's current governing structures, which assumed a more balanced age distribution among the members. Many institutes report that they will not have a sufficient number of members capable of holding a community chapter or able to assume leadership roles in the next ten years. This demographic reality is generating a variety of creative responses—from formal mergers with other institutes, to collaborative efforts in caring and supporting elderly members, to the appointment of guardians or commissaries to care for the elderly members as they diminish.

For a number of the communities based in the United States, but with missions or provinces in other countries, there is a further challenge of a rapidly aging US membership juxtaposed with an increasing membership of younger sisters outside of the United States. How do they negotiate the location of their motherhouse and composition of their leadership? Structures and community habits of inclusion and cultural engagement present practical issues both individually and corporately. The oldest members of a community may have been successful leaders and builders of major apostolic works (universities, schools, hospitals, retreat centers, etc.) that institutionalized the charism and mission of their institutes, but the newer members may now find these institutional responsibilities overwhelming as they discern the charism and mission in more individual and pastoral ministries.

The CARA research reveals sisters responding to these challenges creatively by pursuing innovative collaborations with other religious institutes, with the educational and healthcare ministries previous generations created, and with lay colleagues. Those religious institutes that face great diminishment in number or completion are not passive but are actively pursuing practical strategies to address their reality as women of faith.

At this same time, CARA research identifies new institutes of religious life emerging in the United States and an ever-growing number of religious institutes from Asia, Africa, and Latin America opening new missions in the United States. Whether arising in the United States or coming as missionaries, the newer religious institutes are culturally and ethnically more diverse than existing US institutes and bring charisms rooted in Vietnam, Nigeria, Argentina, and elsewhere. The enrichment and leaven of women religious in the life of the Catholic community in the United States continues as it has for centuries. We draw inspiration from the Letter to the Ephesians 4:3-6, 15-16: "Striv[e] to preserve the unity of the spirit through the bond of peace: one body and one Spirit, as you were also called to the one hope of your call; one Lord, one faith, one baptism; one God and Father of all, who is over all and through all and in all. . . . Rather, living the truth in love, we should grow in every way into him who is the head, Christ, from whom the whole body, joined and held together by every supporting ligament, with the proper functioning of each part, brings about the body's growth and builds itself up in love."

Research Studies Used in This Book

The research incorporated in these pages comes from many different studies of religious life conducted by CARA over the last twenty-five years. While nearly all of the studies involve surveys—of the leaders of religious institutes or of the members and those in formation for these institutes—many of them also include focus groups and interviews, which provide an added richness and depth to the quantitative answers provided by the surveys. Each of the studies is somewhat different, commissioned by a particular client for a particular purpose, with slightly different samples drawn from slightly different populations. Rather than filling the book with extra pages of detailed information about the particular studies, this methodological appendix brings all those details into one spot, for easy comparison of the similarities and differences among the various studies. Organized by the chapter in which each study first appears, the following provides full methodological detail for each study as well as the reference citation for the original study that contains the data. Further information about any of these studies is available from CARA.

Chapter 1: New Members in Religious Life in the United States

This chapter presents data from two major national studies of women religious, conducted ten years apart. The most recent study, commissioned by the National Religious Vocation Conference (NRVC) and conducted by CARA in 2019, was called *Recent Vocations to Religious Life: A Report for the National Religious Vocation Conference*.[1] It largely replicated a 2009 study,[2] also commissioned by NRVC and conducted by CARA, which carried the same title. The studies were designed to identify and understand the characteristics, attitudes, and experiences of the men and women who have entered religious life in recent years.

The 2019 study first surveyed the major superiors of 755 governance units[3] of religious institutes, using lists that were provided to CARA by the Conference of Major Superiors of Men (CMSM), the Council of Major Superiors of Women Religious (CMSWR), and the Leadership Conference of Women Religious (LCWR) as well as lists of superiors of monasteries of contemplative nuns (who do not belong to either LCWR or CMSWR) and emerging communities of consecrated life (from lists compiled by CARA for previous research). The survey (offered in both electronic and paper forms) was administered through spring and summer 2019 and achieved a final response rate of 67 percent (503 respondents for all units). The final response rate for women's religious institutes was also 67 percent (352 units).

Using lists provided by respondents to the survey of major superiors described above, CARA then surveyed the men and women

---

1. Mary L. Gautier and Thu T. Do, *Recent Vocations to Religious Life: A Report for the National Religious Vocation Conference*, A CARA report (Washington, DC: Center for Applied Research in the Apostolate, 2020).

2. Mary E. Bendyna and Mary L. Gautier, *Recent Vocations to Religious Life: A Report for the National Religious Vocation Conference*, A CARA report (Washington, DC: Center for Applied Research in the Apostolate, 2009).

3. A "unit" of an institute is defined as either the congregation as a whole, a governmentally separate province, or an autonomous monastery.

who had entered those institutes in the fifteen years immediately prior to the survey (between 2003 and 2019). The survey (offered in both electronic and paper forms) was distributed in spring and summer 2019 to 3,078 identified new members and those in formation and achieved a final response rate of 63 percent (1,933 respondents). The final response rate among women religious was 71 percent (990 respondents).

In addition to the survey, thirteen focus groups of new members were conducted at various locations throughout the country during fall 2019. Participants were selected from among the survey respondents who indicated that they would be willing to participate in a focus group and included women and men, ordained and nonordained, contemplative and active, and professed members as well as those in formation. The focus groups were designed to allow for more in-depth responses from new members about the attractions and challenges of religious life.

The 2009 study utilized the same methodology as was used in the 2019 study, with the sole exception that the 2009 surveys were not available to respondents in electronic form. The 2009 survey of major superiors was mailed to the major superiors of 976 units of men and women religious (251 units of men religious from CMSM lists, 467 units of women religious from LCWR and CMSWR lists, and 258 monasteries of contemplative nuns and emerging communities from CARA lists). The survey was administered in spring and summer 2008 and achieved a final response rate of 60 percent (591 responses for all units). The final response rate for women's religious institutes was also 60 percent (429 units).

The 2009 survey of new members was mailed to 3,965 new members who had been identified by their major superior. The survey was administered in fall 2008 through winter 2009. After removing undeliverable addresses and other unusable names from the dataset, the final response rate for new members was approximately 40 percent (1,568 usable responses). The final response rate for women religious new members was 45 percent (985 usable responses).

A limited amount of additional information on the family and religious backgrounds of women religious was compiled for this chapter from data collected annually by CARA for *Women and Men Entering Religious Life: The Entrance Class of [Year]* and *Women and Men Professing Perpetual Vows in Religious Life: The Profession Class of [Year].* These have been conducted annually by CARA since 2012, with funding for the Entrance Class study provided by the Conrad N. Hilton Foundation and funding for the Profession Class study provided by the United States Conference of Catholic Bishops. The methodology for these two studies is similar to that for the NRVC studies described above, employing an annual survey of men and women identified by the superior of their institute as either entering their institute or professing perpetual vows in their institute each calendar year. Approximately 60 to 75 percent of religious institutes provide these names each year, and at least two-thirds of identified entrants and newly professed members participate in the respective surveys.

For the purpose of chapter 1, the above described data from all datasets were reanalyzed to focus exclusively on women's religious institutes and women religious.

Chapter 2: Cultural Diversity in Vocations to Religious Life in the United States

This chapter presents data from a 2021 CARA study called *Cultural Diversity in Vocations to Religious Life in the United States: A National Study of New Religious Members.*[4] This study was conducted by CARA in 2020, with funding from the Conrad N. Hilton Foundation. It investigated the impact of parishes and family life on the vocational discernment of religious members before they entered religious life to explore possible cultural differences

---

4. Thu T. Do, Jonathon L. Wiggins, Thomas P. Gaunt, *Cultural Diversity in Vocations to Religious Life in the United States: A National Study of New Religious Members*, A CARA report (Washington, DC: Center for Applied Research in the Apostolate, 2021).

in those experiences. The study also explored the experiences of cultural diversity in religious institutes among new members and what members from the nondominant culture or ethnicity experience as challenges within their religious institute.

Using contact information requested from the major superiors of religious institutes in the United States, CARA invited 3,196 identified current candidates/postulants, novices, and those in temporary vows as well as those identified members who had professed perpetual vows within the last fifteen years. A total of ninety-nine invitees declined to participate for various reasons. The survey was administered in spring and summer 2020 and concluded with a final response rate of 38 percent (1,163 usable responses). The final response for women religious new members was 48 percent (600 usable responses). For the purpose of chapter 2, the dataset was reanalyzed using only the data from women religious.

Chapter 3: International Religious Institutes in the United States

This chapter presents data from a CARA study called *International Religious Institutes Present in the United States since 1965*.[5] This study was conducted by CARA in 2020, with generous funding from the Conrad N. Hilton Foundation. It investigated the religious institutes that were founded outside the United States but have had a presence in the United States since 1965. This presence could be in the form of a mission ministry, province, or region that may or may not belong to their original religious institutes in their home countries in terms of governance. The data collected for the study come from a survey of 384 religious institutes identified by the chancellor or vicar for religious in 128 US arch/dioceses as meeting the criteria for inclusion in the study. The survey was

5. Thu T. Do and Thomas P. Gaunt, *International Religious Institutes Present in the United States since 1965*, A CARA report (Washington, DC: Center for Applied Research in the Apostolate, 2020).

administered during spring and summer 2020 and concluded with a final response rate of 56 percent (215 respondents) for all units. Of these responding units, 163 are units of women religious, which were separately analyzed for the purpose of chapter 3.

Chapter 5: The Evolution of Leadership in Religious Life

The findings presented in chapter 5 are based on the CARA study called *Forming a New Generation of Leadership for Religious Institutes*.[6] This study was conducted by CARA in 2019, with generous funding from the Conrad N. Hilton Foundation. It investigated the evolution of leadership in US-based religious institutes, from the perspective of the superior who is in charge of a unit. The data collected for the study come from a national survey (offered in both electronic and paper forms) of all major superiors of religious institutes in the United States. The survey was administered from the beginning of December 2018 until the end of January 2019. The survey concluded with a final response rate of 58 percent (418 respondents) for all institutes (women, men, contemplative, and unidentified). The response rate for the women's religious institutes was 63 percent (248 units). Notably, those who returned the survey completed, on average, only 77 percent of the questions. This relatively low completion rate can be explained by the fact that 13 percent of those who responded to the survey indicated that they no longer accept new members, and so the majority of the questions did not apply to them.

In addition to the survey, four focus groups and three individual interviews were conducted with the leaders of men's and women's religious institutes at several locations throughout the Midwestern United States during summer and fall 2019. These focus groups and interviews were selected to obtain the views of

6. Patricia A. Wittberg et al., *Forming a New Generation of Leadership for Religious Institutes*, A CARA report (Washington, DC: Center for Applied Research in the Apostolate, 2019).

leaders of institutes whose international presence and leadership have taken a variety of different forms. For the purpose of chapter 5, the above described data were reanalyzed focusing exclusively on women's religious institutes.

Chapter 6: Restructuring Governance in Religious Life

This chapter presents findings drawn from several studies of religious institutes conducted by CARA in 2019 and 2020. The first study cited in the chapter is called *Experiences of Women Religious Congregations Engaged in Renewing Their Governance Structures*.[7] This study was conducted by CARA, in collaboration with CommunityWorks, Inc., with generous funding from the Conrad N. Hilton Foundation. It investigated eight institutes of women religious who were in the process of discerning or implementing a new governance structure for their institute. The institutes selected for the study included three suggested by CommunityWorks, Inc., who are working with that organization in a process for reenvisioning their governance structures to better support the life and mission of the sisters in each institute. The other five institutes were selected in consultation with the Union of International Superiors General (UISG) and are known by them to be in the process of restructuring their governance. The data collected for the study come from two surveys designed by CARA (one for institutes discerning a new governance structure and the other for those implementing a new governance structure) and distributed to thirty-eight key informants of those institutes who were selected by their superiors for the experience with the institute's governance restructuring process. A total of thirty-three key informants responded to the questionnaires: fifteen respondents from four institutes that are discerning a new governance structure and

7. Thu T. Do, Thomas P. Gaunt, and Jonathon L. Wiggins, *Experiences of Women Religious Congregations Engaged in Renewing Their Governance Structures*, A CARA report (Washington, DC: Center for Applied Research in the Apostolate, 2020).

eighteen respondents from four institutes that are implementing a new governance structure.

A second study cited in this chapter is called *Governance Structure: Survey of Members of the Leadership Conference of Women Religious*.[8] This study was commissioned by the Leadership Conference of Women Religious and conducted by CARA in 2019 and 2020. It investigated changes in LCWR member institutes' governing structures. LCWR designed a questionnaire and sent it to all member institutes following a video on governance and restructuring. The survey was administered by LCWR from November 2019 through January 2020. The survey concluded with a response rate of 70 percent (212 member institutes). CARA conducted the analysis of the data and prepared a report of the findings.

The third and final study cited in this chapter is called *The Challenges Facing Small, Aging US Women's Religious Institutes with Limited Resources: Findings from the Focus Groups*.[9] The study was commissioned by Support Our Aging Religious! (SOAR!) and conducted by CARA in April 2021. It investigated the challenges that small, aging US women's religious institutes with limited resources face and drew out insights about what solutions those institutes envision to address those challenges. The data collected for the study are drawn from two focus groups with major superiors and other selected leaders from a sample of women's religious institutes. SOAR! provided names of twenty major superiors whose congregations met the criteria for inclusion in the focus groups: small religious institutes of women whose members are primarily elderly sisters with very limited resources. Ten of the congregations have motherhouses in the eastern United States,

---

8. Thu T. Do, Jonathon L. Wiggins, and Thomas P. Gaunt, *Governance Structure: Survey of Members of the Leadership Conference of Women Religious*, A CARA report (Washington, DC: Center for Applied Research in the Apostolate, 2020).

9. Jonathon L. Wiggins and Thomas P. Gaunt, *The Challenges Facing Small, Aging US Women's Religious Institutes with Limited Resources: Findings from the Focus Groups*, A CARA report (Washington, DC: Center for Applied Research in the Apostolate, 2021).

and ten have motherhouses in the southern and western United States. CARA e-mailed an invitation to the leaders of the twenty congregations, and a total of ten participated in the two focus groups. The focus groups were conducted by Zoom (partially due to the current Covid-19 pandemic) and were recorded by CARA.

References

Annuarium Statisticum Ecclesiae (Statistical Yearbook of the Church). Rome: Libreria Editrice Vaticana, 1970–2019.

Arbuckle, Gerald. *Out of Chaos: Refounding Religious Congregations*. New York: Paulist Press, 1988.

Bader, Janice. "Canonical Governance Options and Opportunities for Collaboration." *RCRI Bulletin* 24 (Winter 2020–2021).

Bendyna, Mary E., and Mary L. Gautier. *Recent Vocations to Religious Life: A Report for the National Religious Vocation Conference*. A CARA report. Washington, DC: Center for Applied Research in the Apostolate, 2009.

Byrne, Patricia. "Sisters of St. Joseph: The Americanization of a French Tradition." *U.S. Catholic Historian* 5, nos. 3–4 (1986): 241–72.

Cada, Lawrence, Raymond Fitz, Gertrude Foley, Thomas Giardino, and Carol Lichtenberg. *Shaping the Coming Age of Religious Life*. New York: Seabury Press, 1979.

Center for Applied Research in the Apostolate. *Emerging US Communities of Consecrated Life since Vatican II*. 3rd ed. Washington, DC: Center for Applied Research in the Apostolate, 2017.

Congregation for Institutes of Consecrated Life and Societies of Apostolic Life. *New Wine in New Wineskins: The Consecrated Life and Its Ongoing Challenges since Vatican II*. Rome: Libreria Editrice Vaticana, 2017.

Coriden, James A., Thomas J. Green, and Donald E. Heintschel. *The Code of Canon Law: A Text and Commentary*. New York: Paulist Press, 1985.

Do, Thu T., and Mary L. Gautier. *International Religious Sisters Studying in the United States*. A CARA report. Washington, DC: Center for Applied Research in the Apostolate, 2018.

Do, Thu T., and Thomas P. Gaunt. *International Religious Institutes Present in the United States since 1965*. A CARA report. Washington, DC: Center for Applied Research in the Apostolate, 2020.

Do, Thu T., Jonathon L. Wiggins, and Thomas P. Gaunt. *Cultural Diversity in Vocations to Religious Life in the United States: A National Study of New Religious Members*. A CARA report. Washington, DC: Center for Applied Research in the Apostolate, 2021.

Do, Thu T., Jonathon L. Wiggins, and Thomas P. Gaunt. *Governance Structure: Survey of Members of the Leadership Conference of Women Religious*. A CARA report. Washington, DC: Center for Applied Research in the Apostolate, 2020.

Do, Thu T., Thomas P. Gaunt, and Jonathon L. Wiggins. *Experiences of Women Religious Congregations Engaged in Renewing Their Governance Structures*. A CARA report. Washington, DC: Center for Applied Research in the Apostolate, 2020.

Engh, Michael E. *Frontier Faiths: Church, Temple, and Synagogue in Los Angeles, 1846–1888*. Albuquerque: University of New Mexico Press, 1992.

Euart, Sharon A. "Canonical Governance: Commissary of a Religious Institute." In *Roman Replies and CLSA Advisory Opinions 2018*. Edited by Sharon A. Euart and John A. Alesandro. Washington, DC: CLSA, 2018.

Euart, Sharon A. "Canonical Governance Options and Opportunities for Collaboration." *RCRI Bulletin* 24 (Winter 2020–2021).

Ewens, Mary. "Women in the Convent." In *American Catholic Women: A Historical Exploration*, edited by Karen Kennelly, 17–47. New York: Macmillan, 1989.

Gautier, Mary L., and Thu T. Do. *Recent Vocations to Religious Life: A Report for the National Religious Vocation Conference*. A CARA report. Washington, DC: Center for Applied Research in the Apostolate, 2020.

Gray, Mark M., Mary L. Gautier, and Thomas P. Gaunt. *Cultural Diversity in the Catholic Church in the United States*. Washington, DC: Center for Applied Research in the Apostolate, 2014.

Greenwood, Julia, and Mary Gautier. *Trends in the Life and Ministry of Religious Sisters in Latin America: A CARA Special Report*. Washington, DC: Center for Applied Research in the Apostolate, 2018.

Hereford, Amy. "CANON 580: Aggregation and Covenants." In *Roman Replies and CLSA Advisory Opinions 2012*, edited by Sharon A. Euart, John A. Alesandro, and Thomas J. Green. Washington, DC: Canon Law Society of America, 2012.

Hereford, Amy. *Navigating Change: The Role of Law in the Life-Cycle of a Religious Institute*. St. Louis, MO: Religious Life Project, 2014.

Hereford, Amy. *Religious Life at the Crossroads*. Maryknoll, NY: Orbis Books, 2013.

Holland, Sharon. "New Institutes, Mergers, and Supression." In *Procedural Handbook for Institutes of Consecrated Life and Societies of Apostolic Life*, edited by Michael Joyce. Washington, DC: Canon Law Society of America, 2001.

Jarrell, Lynn. "The Roles of the Religious Institute and the Diocesan Bishop When the Institute Is Facing the Reality of Decline." *CLSA Proceedings* 80 (2019).

Johnson, Mary, Mary L. Gautier, Patricia Wittberg, and Thu T. Do. *Migration for Mission: International Catholic Sisters in the United States*. New York: Oxford University Press, 2019.

Karimi, Kevin, Michael J. DeFelice, Thomas P. Gaunt, and Mary L. Gautier. *Special Report on International Women Religious in the United States*. Washington, DC: Center for Applied Research in the Apostolate, 2019.

Korte, Lyn. "Canonical Governance Options and Opportunities for Collaboration." *RCRI Bulletin* 24 (Winter 2020–2021).

Lacour, Ann. "Canonical Governance Options and Opportunities for Collaboration." *RCRI Bulletin* 24 (Winter 2020–2021).

Mannard, Joseph G. "Maternity . . . of the Spirit: Nuns and Domesticity in Antebellum America." *U.S. Catholic Historian* 5, nos. 3–4 (1986): 305–24.

Mbonu, Caroline N. "Reversed Missionary Action: Prospects and Challenges for African Women Religious." *Religious Life Review* (July/August, 2016): 217–28.

McDermott, Patricia. "Canonical Governance Options and Opportunities for Collaboration." *RCRI Bulletin* 24 (Winter 2020–2021).

McDermott, Rose. "Institutes of Consecrated Life and Societies of Apostolic Life." In *New Commentary on the Code of Canon Law*, edited by John P. Beal, James A. Coriden, and Thomas J. Green. Mahwah, NJ: Paulist Press, 2000.

McNamara, Jo Ann Kay. *Sisters in Arms: Catholic Nuns through Two Millennia*. Cambridge, MA: Harvard University Press, 1996.

Nygren, David J., and Miriam D. Ukeritis. *The Future of Religious Orders in the United States: Transformation and Commitment*. Westport, CT: Praeger, 1993.

The Official Catholic Directory. Berkeley Heights, NJ: P. J. Kenedy & Sons, 1966.

Pope Francis. Apostolic exhortation *Evangelii Gaudium.* Rome: November 24, 2013.

Pope John Paul II. Post-synodal apostolic exhortation *Vita Consecrata.* Rome: March 25, 1996.

Pope Paul VI. Apostolic letter *Ecclesiae Sanctae.* Rome: August 6, 1966.

Pope Paul VI. Decree on the Adaptation and Renewal of Religious Life *Perfectae Caritatis.* Rome: October 28, 1965.

Rapley, Elizabeth. *The Lord as Their Portion: The Story of the Religious Orders and How They Shaped Our World.* Grand Rapids: Eerdmans, 2011.

Still, Stephanie. "Canonical Governance Options and Possibilities for Collaboration." *RCRI Bulletin* 24 (Winter 2020–2021).

Stockman, Dan. "Collaborative Governance Model Helps Congregations Carry on with Limited Resources." *Global Sisters Report.* February 12, 2018.

Thompson, Margaret Susan. "Sisterhood and Power: Class, Culture, and Ethnicity in the American Convent." *Colby Library Quarterly* 25, no. 3 (September 1989).

Wiggins, Jonathon L., and Thomas P. Gaunt. *The Challenges Facing Small, Aging US Women's Religious Institutes with Limited Resources: Findings from the Focus Groups.* A CARA report. Washington, DC: Center for Applied Research in the Apostolate, 2021.

Wittberg, Patricia. "The Influences of Families on Religious Vocations." In *Pathways to Religious Life,* edited by Thomas Gaunt, 37–59. New York: Oxford University Press, 2018.

Wittberg, Patricia. *The Rise and Fall of Catholic Religious Orders: A Social Movement Perspective.* Albany: SUNY Press, 1994.

Wittberg, Patricia A., Michal J. Kramarek, Mary L. Gautier, Thu T. Do, and Felice M. Goodwin. *Forming a New Generation of Leadership for Religious Institutes.* A CARA report. Washington, DC: Center for Applied Research in the Apostolate, 2019.

Index